D1548255

The Smell of War

NUMBER FOURTEEN
C. A. Brannen Series

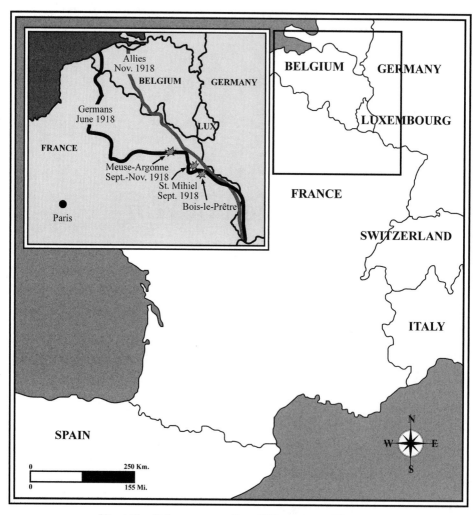

**Battle Lines on the Western Front
June–November 1918**

Map by Alex Mendoza

The Smell of War

THREE AMERICANS IN THE TRENCHES OF WORLD WAR I

Edited with Commentary
by Virginia Bernhard

TEXAS A&M UNIVERSITY PRESS
COLLEGE STATION

Library of Congress Cataloging-in-Publication Control Number: 2017023519

In memory of all who lost their lives in the Great War

Contents

Illustrations

Photographs

Maps

Preface

Until recently, I knew next to nothing about World War I except what I taught to college freshmen in my US history survey. I was a colonial American historian, working mainly in seventeenth-century sources. Then I detoured into the nineteenth and early twentieth centuries with the Hoggs of Texas. When I discovered Mike Hogg's World War I letters, I knew they had to see print—and then one thing led to another. In the course of editing Mike Hogg's letters, I came across the "smell of war" quotation by Henry Sheahan and the history of the 90th Division by George Wythe. When I realized that all three of these young men had connections with one small battlefield in the Great War, I knew their stories could be a book.

Framed by the larger history of World War I, this work is a micro-history of that conflict. What happened from 1914 to 1918 on a three-square-mile patch of land in northeastern France captures the whole history of the war. This place was called the *Bois-le-Prêtre* by the French and *der Priesterwald* by the Germans. In English it means "Priest's Wood." It was heavily forested, and during the war it came to be known as the "Wood of Death." Hundreds of thousands of soldiers—French, German, and some American—fought and died there. The exact numbers will never be known.

Possession of the Bois-le-Prêtre was a key to controlling a major rail line and thus one key to winning the war. It was a bloody battleground off and on for four years, until American and French troops seized it in September 1918.

What took place in the Bois-le-Prêtre is what took place on the whole Western Front. From the ambulance drivers who often drove for days and nights without sleep, under fire and over unfamiliar terrain during pitch-dark nights, to the soldiers who went "over the top" against enemy guns time after time and came back (the lucky ones) to the mud and rats and lice in the trenches, to the dogged military strategists who did their best to win on battlefronts that stretched for miles, World War I was like no other war.

From Henry Sheahan, the volunteer ambulance driver, we learn what Paris was like in 1915, when French soldiers on leave sat in cafés and talked of war. We ride with him on his first ambulance run, when 20,000 wounded each night for three nights were brought in on trains to a suburb of Paris to be ferried to hospitals and houses. We learn from Sheahan what it was like to see a man hit by a bullet fall slowly to the ground and die. We share a moment of joy with him when he plays an old piano to accompany a youthful violinist whose instrument is made from a cigar box. Fluent in French, Henry Sheahan captured the war as it came to soldiers and villagers, and what he wrote in English is a sensitive, lyrical, and at times disturbingly literal account of what he saw. He left the American Field Service after the battle of Verdun in 1916, saddened and disillusioned. His memoir, *A Volunteer Poilu*, was first published in October 1916.

Mike Hogg, whose cheery letters home serve as a kind of antidote to the horrors of war, served as the captain of Company D, 1st Battalion, 360th Infantry, 180th Brigade, 90th Division. He wrote to his sister, Ima Hogg, and to his brother, Will, with vivid details of his experiences, from listening to "the darn fool civilians, who have singing societies, or think they can sing," at Camp Travis; to learning French while training for combat on the Western Front: "I have a beautiful pronunciation, but alas, no memory. The darn stuff goes in one ear and out the other"; to being in battle: "This is about one week since the beginning and we are still fighting. . . . Many of my men have not yet had their clothes off and of course the shelling continues here and there." Slightly wounded in the Battle of St. Mihiel, he rejoined his men in active combat until the armistice of November 11, 1918, and served in the Army of Occupation after that. He did not come home until April 1919.

George Wythe, like Mike Hogg, trained at Camp Travis and fought on the Western Front. A former journalist, Major Wythe was chosen to write the official history of the 90th Division immediately after the war. His account serves as a backdrop for Mike Hogg's letters, with details that might otherwise have been lost: "No one who has ever taken a look at No Man's Land on this front, and seen that twisting, treacherous mass of [barbed] wire . . . has failed to ask how it was possible for human beings to cross such obstacles in the face of hostile fire. . . . French staff officers . . . gasped in astonishment when they heard of the facility with which American doughboys had surmounted such seemingly unconquerable difficulties. . . . But it is sufficient to say that these men from the Southwest were natives of barbed wire's native States!" When wire cutters proved too slow, many soldiers flung them aside, and "the bands [of wire] were cleared at one leap . . . the clothes of hundreds were torn to shreds, and some arrived . . . so naked that it was necessary to send them to the rear for a new uniform in order to avoid freezing." Major Wythe wrote his history in May and June 1919 and returned to the United States in August 1919.

What Henry Sheahan, Mike Hogg, and George Wythe left us is one small part of the history of the Great War.

Acknowledgments

As the editor of this book, my first thanks must go to Henry Sheahan, Mike Hogg, and George Wythe, the three authors whose works made it possible. For permission to publish Mike Hogg's letters, which first appeared in the *Southwestern Historical Quarterly* 117, no. 1 (July 2013) and no. 2 (October 2013), I thank that journal and its staff, especially editor Mike Campbell and associate editor Ryan Schumacher, who steered my manuscript past many errors. Another note of gratitude is due to serendipity: Alan Garrett, professor of education at Eastern New Mexico University, happened to see Mike Hogg's war letters in print and sent me a congratulatory email. In it he mentioned that his great-uncle, Joseph C. Garrett, had fought in Company D, Mike Hogg's company, and was kind enough to send me copies of his great-uncle's papers, including a faded typescript titled "History of Company D, 180th Infantry." Excerpts from that document are part of this book, thanks to Alan Garrett.

My research owes much to the staffs of several institutions: Margaret Schlankey and others at the Dolph Briscoe Center for American History at the University of Texas at Austin; Lorraine Stewart and the archives staff at the Museum of Fine Arts, Houston; the staff at the Clayton Library Center for Genealogical Research in Houston, and Kat Stefko and Sophie Mendoza of the Bowdoin College Library in Brunswick, Maine. Thanks also to Don Wilding, author of the blog capecodonline.com; and Peter J. W. Folkers, whose online photos taught me much about the Bois le Prêtre. I also thank the staff of Doherty Library at the University of St. Thomas in Houston, especially the interlibrary loan expert, Reverend George Hosko.

Special thanks to my colleagues Sam Watson and Roswitha Wagner; and to Pat Clabaugh, associate editor at Texas A&M University

Press; Cynthia Lindlof, copyeditor; and Alex Mendoza, mapmaker. Jim Bernhard, my husband, faithful reader, and fearless critic, went through several versions of this work and listened patiently to my countless World War I stories. He knows how much I owe him.

—Houston, Texas, January 2017

Note on Sources

Henry Sheahan's World War I journal was published as *A Volunteer Poilu* (Boston: Houghton Mifflin, 1916). *The Smell of War* uses a 1916 reprint of the original edition, available at https://www.amazon.com/RE-PRINT-volunteer-1888–1968-VERSION-ORIGINAL/dp/B004G4W1TO/ref=sr_1_1?s=books&ie=UTF8&qid=1485277145&sr=1–1&keywords=a+volunteer+poilu+by+henry+beston.

Elmer Stetson Harden, a Sheahan contemporary, edited a later version, *An American Poilu* (Boston: Little, Brown, 1919).

There are three recent editions: Henry Sheahan, *A Volunteer Poilu* (Gloucester, UK: Dodo Press, 2007; New York: Tutis Digital Publishing, 2008; and Amazon CreateSpace Independent Publishing Platform, 2016).

Sheahan also wrote a journal piece, "One of the Sections at Verdun," included in A. Piatt Andrew's anthology, *Friends of France: The Field Service of the American Ambulance Described by Its Members* (New York: Houghton Mifflin, 1916). See the online version, *V: The Section in Lorraine*, http://www.gwpda.org/medical/FriendsFrance/ff02.htm.

Mike Hogg's war letters exist only in a bound typescript edited by his sister, Ima Hogg, and presented to him as a gift. This bound volume is in the Museum of Fine Arts Archives, Houston. There is also a copy in the Hogg Collections at the Dolph Briscoe Center for American History at the University of Texas at Austin. Mike Hogg claimed that he wrote to his sister "every week" from May 1917 to April 1919, except for the weeks he was in active service on the Western Front, but if he did, all of his letters have not survived. To date, the originals of his letters have not been located.

George Wythe, who served with distinction as a young officer from June 1917 to August 1919, was promoted to major on October

13, 1918, just days before the November 11 Armistice. After the war's end, he was chosen to write the history of the 90th Division in which he served. The result, after a year's work, was *A History of the 90th Division* (New York: 90th Division Association, 1920).

Wythe's book exists in several editions and an online version: http://www.90thdivisionassoc.org/history/UnitHistories/index. html.

A recent version, reprinted from the original 1920 edition, is *A History of the 90th Division* (Delhi, India: Reink Books, 2015), https:// www.abebooks.com/book-search/title/history-90th-division/.

In this book, some instances of the authors' spelling and punctuation have been corrected for clarity.

The Smell of War

The "Wood of Death"
1914–1918

The war has a smell that clings to everything military, fills the troop-trains, hospitals, and cantonments, and saturates one's own clothing, a smell compounded of horse, chemicals, sweat, mud, dirt, and human beings.

—Henry Sheahan, *A Volunteer Poilu*, 1916

An American ambulance driver for the French wrote these words about a war that happened a hundred years ago. Trees that were turned to sawdust by mortar shells have now grown back, but craters from mine explosions, some nearly thirty yards deep, still pockmark the earth on old battlefields in France. One of these is a forest called the *Bois-le-Prêtre* (Priest's Wood). The Germans called it *der Priesterwald*. It is located on the west bank of the Moselle River, just north of the town of Montauville in Lorraine, and it was a battleground for four years. Coils of rusty barbed wire still stretch through undergrowth in what was once "No Man's Land," and holes now overgrown with leaves lead to deep underground bunkers. In a rubble of bricks and stones that was once a village, there is a weather-beaten stone monument with this inscription:

IN MEMORY OF OUR ANCESTORS
WHOSE GRAVES HAVE BEEN DISTURBED
DURING THE WAR 1914–1918.
A GROUP OF INHABITANTS OF FEY-EN-HAYE.

Fey-en-Haye once had 150 residents. They lived at the edge of the Bois-le-Prêtre, or "Wood of Death," as it came to be called. This massive forest, covering three square miles, was the scene of some of the deadliest fighting of World War I. Besides Fey-en-Haye, two other

"A Madman's Maze": The Bois-le-Prêtre in 1915. Source: http://pierreswestern front.punt.nl/.

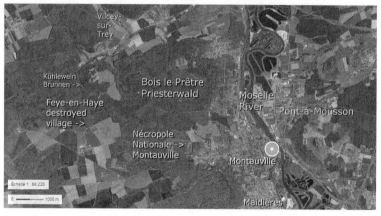

Aerial view of the Bois-le-Prêtre and Fey-en-Haye. Source: http://pierreswesternfront.punt.nl/.

small villages, Reniéville and Remenauville, were also destroyed. Possession of the Bois-le-Prêtre meant control of a crucial railroad line at nearby St. Mihiel. In 1914 the Germans took the Bois-le-Prêtre; the French kept trying to get it back, year after year. Rows of white crosses and monuments to the unknown dead testify to the killings on this ground. Exact totals may never be known. For example, one partial count is on a stone marker:

Ruins of the village of Fey-en-Haye. Source: http://pierreswesternfront.punt.nl/.

On this line of ridges from January to August 1915 the 73rd and
128th Divisions have lost 7,000 dead and 22,000 wounded.
The Germans have experienced equivalent losses.
Passer-by, Respect this sacred soil.[1]

The Americans finally took the Bois-le-Prêtre from the Germans in
fierce fighting at the Battle of St. Mihiel in 1918.[2]

Henry Sheahan described the Wood of Death as "a madman's
maze of barbed wire, earthy lines, trenches—some of them untenable
by either side and still full of the dead who fell in the last combat—
shell holes, and fortified craters." Sheahan drove an ambulance there
in 1915. George Wythe and Mike Hogg fought there in 1918, and it
looked just the same. All three young men would write about it later.[3]

The Coming of War, 1914

World War I was a war that no one in 1914 wanted to happen. After all, this was the twentieth century, and war was outmoded. Civilized nations were to settle their differences by diplomacy, not cannons and rifles. Two international conferences in 1899 and 1907 at The Hague, Netherlands, the first proposed by Russian czar Nicholas II and the second spearheaded by American president Theodore Roosevelt, had laid down the rules: Under the Hague Conventions, deadly weapons of destruction such as bombs dropped from the air (the Wright brothers had flown an airplane successfully in 1903), chemical warfare, and certain kinds of bullets were banned.[1]

But in the summer of 1914 war came, and from 1914 to 1918 it mobilized more than 65 million men from nations around the globe. It killed 8,528,831 (including 53,513 Americans) and wounded 21,159,154 (204,002 of them were Americans).[2] The numbers of troops killed and the rounds of ammunition fired were counted in the millions. Airplanes, tanks, machine guns, and poison gas flouted the Hague Conventions. That war was called the "Great War." In the first decades of the twentieth century, no one could imagine a war that would be greater. In the first decades of the twenty-first century, we can see the origins of World War II, the Cold War, and even terrorism in World War I and its aftermath.

On July 11, 1914, a young woman named Ima Hogg sailed from Galveston, Texas, on the *Chemnitz*, a German ship bound for the port of Bremerhaven, Germany. She was the only daughter of James Stephen Hogg, governor of Texas from 1891 to 1895. It was he who had given her that improbable name, for reasons that to this day remain unclear.[3] Her voyage was to be a fateful one. Two weeks before the *Chemnitz* sailed, diplomatic dominoes across Europe had begun to tumble down. On June 28, Archduke Franz Ferdinand, the heir to the Austro-Hungarian throne, and his wife, Duchess Sophie, had been killed by a Serbian assassin in Sarajevo (a day that also happened to be the couple's wedding anniversary). Neither Ima Hogg nor her friends nor anyone else could believe that the great powers of Europe, bound by networks of civility and diplomacy, would suddenly declare war on each other. George V of England, Czar Nicholas II of Russia, and Kaiser Wilhelm of Germany were first cousins: they were the grandsons of Queen Victoria. No one imagined that a single assassination would topple the elaborate house of foreign policy cards that had kept Europe relatively stable since the Franco-Prussian War in 1870. But after the Sarajevo assassination, Austria declared war against Serbia. This offended Russia, a defender of Serbia. A complicated relationship quickly drew in the two major alliances whose members were pledged to support each other: Austria-Hungary, Germany, and Italy (the Triple Alliance, later joined by Turkey and Bulgaria) against England, France, and Russia (the Triple Entente). On July 28, one month after the assassination in Sarajevo, Austria declared war on Serbia, and the slide into war began.

On July 29, Ima Hogg, still at sea, sent a cable from the *Chemnitz* to her home in Houston: "When news came of the Austro-Serbian conflict and the Triple-Alliance complications, our imaginations even pictured us being captured by an English cruiser in the Channel!" Traveling with friends, she was not really alarmed. "The latest news," she wrote, "makes us think all will be peaceably settled."[4]

On July 30, Russia prepared for war against Austria-Hungary and Germany. On August 1, Germany declared war on Russia. That was the day that the *Chemnitz* docked in Bremerhaven. Passengers who had looked forward to a late-summer holiday in Germany were quickly rerouted. On August 3 Germany declared war on France, and on that day Ima Hogg and many others sailed on the *St. Petersburgh*, bound for England.[5] As soon as she arrived in London, Ima sent another cablegram home: "The situation on the Continent is already frightful, even if nothing more happens, and I am sure more is to come of it. However, none of us are sorry we came. We were among the last of two ships to be allowed in the North Sea and to land in Germany." The voyage from Germany to England was "a terrible trip, yet still without discourtesies. . . . A great many things happened—lack of food, crushes of people, no place to sleep. . . . We bade goodbye, ourselves, to many stalwart, handsome fellows. The tragedy is like nothing I can imagine. In Bremen, everything seemed suspended—people gathered in small groups—in hushed voices, talking eagerly. Here [in London], it is the same."[6]

This cable is dated August 4. That was the day England declared war on Germany. But Ima wrote later, on August 25, "Poor Germany—my heart just aches for her. Anybody who knows Germany and the Germans is bound to sympathize."[7] Ima Hogg did, and so did many other Americans. As children Ima and her brothers had learned German prayers at the knee of their mother's Bavarian maid. As an aspiring concert pianist, Ima had recently spent most of 1908 studying piano in Berlin. Since then she had returned three times to Germany, once with her brother Mike—who would soon return to Germany under quite different circumstances. Now, as Europe went to war in late August, Ima and many other American tourists were stranded abroad. The earliest passage home that she could book was on the New York American Line's *St. Paul,* sailing on September 16.[8]

Ships might be delayed, but the war did not wait. By August 5 Germany had invaded Belgium. Before Ima Hogg sailed for home, a huge German army had plunged through Belgium into northern France, trying to outflank the French forces and capture Paris from behind. From September 5 through September 12 the armies fought near the Marne River in what would be called the First Battle of the Marne, involving more than 2 million men and 500,000 total dead and wounded.[9]

World War I was the first modern war: the first war to use tanks, airplanes, and heavy artillery that could fire a shell sixty miles. Such destructive power produced devastating losses of life and limb. Another modern invention, the automobile, proved unexpectedly useful. Not only could it carry officers quickly to strategic command posts; it could transport wounded soldiers to hospitals behind the battle lines. Instead of horses and wagons, motorized ambulances could now bring the thousands of casualties to relative safety. In September 1914 a small group of Americans living in Paris and stunned by the terrible carnage at the Marne, volunteered to help the French. On September 7, 1914, the first convoy of volunteer drivers in the hastily formed American Ambulance Service left for duty at the battlefront. These drivers were the first, but there would be many more to come.[10]

These ambulance drivers were volunteers. Most Americans at

home, including Henry Sheahan, George Wythe, and Mike Hogg, followed the war's progress with grave concern but with little thought
of America's involvement. The United States was officially a neutral
nation until 1917. This was Europe's war, not America's, but news of
it continued to shock: In October 1914 the Battle of Ypres (the British liked to call it "Wipers"), a Belgian city, cost 210,000 casualties;
in April and May 1915 the Second Battle of Ypres resulted in 200,000
more and the first major use of chemical warfare by the Germans.[11]
(The Allies, including the Americans, would use it later.) On May 7,
1915, a German U-boat torpedoed the British passenger liner *Lusitania*
off the coast of Ireland. The *Lusitania* went down rapidly, along with
1,200 people—128 of them Americans. The disaster outraged Americans, and many called for war. Anti-German hysteria swept over the
country. President Woodrow Wilson sent a stern protest to Germany,
and for a while German U-boats were ordered not to fire on passenger liners. That order would not last long. Desperate measures were
needed to win a war that turned into a stalemate.

From September to November 1914, the opposing armies dug in.
A line of battle trenches opened like a gash across Europe from the
North Sea to the border of Switzerland. From these trenches (including those in the Bois-le-Prêtre) Allied and German troops would face
each other on the Western Front in a bloody standoff for the next four
years. On the Eastern Front on the plains of eastern Europe, Russian
and German armies were also fighting, but the Germans were winning.

Most Americans remained on the sidelines, but not all. In December 1914 an American named A. Piatt Andrew, a former US assistant
secretary of the treasury who had also taught economics at Harvard,
organized the American Ambulance Field Service (later to become the
American Field Service, AFS) to provide ambulances for the American Hospital in Paris. By April 1915 the AFS sections were attached
to French army divisions. Young Americans, including many college
students, eagerly volunteered for service. Before the war ended, 2,500
AFS ambulance drivers had carried 500,000 wounded to safety.[12]

One of these drivers was Henry Sheahan.

The Ambulance Driver
1915–1916

Henry Sheahan was fluent in French. He had learned it from his French-born mother and polished it when he taught at the University of Lyon in Lyon, France, two years before the war. In 1914 Sheahan was in Cambridge, Massachusetts. He had returned to his alma mater, Harvard, where he earned a BA in 1909 and his MA in 1911. Now he was a young instructor in the Department of English. When war broke out in Europe and France began to mobilize against Germany, one of Sheahan's colleagues, Charles Copeland, encouraged him and other young men "to go over and help" in any way that they could.[1] That opportunity came from the work of another Harvard professor, A. Piatt Andrew, founder of the American Field Service. AFS groups of volunteer ambulance drivers in specially made Fords were now attached to French line divisions, and by September 1915 Henry Sheahan, age twenty-seven, had signed up. Handsome, dark-haired, and single (he did not marry until he was forty-one), he was also a gifted writer.

He knew Paris from his earlier time in France, but he did not know it in a time of war. On Sunday, September 25, awaiting his first assignment, he wandered around the city he loved.

It was Sunday morning, the bells were ringing to church, and I was strolling in the gardens of the Tuileries. A bright morning sun was drying the dewy lawns and the wet marble bodies of the gods and athletes, the leaves on the trees were falling, and the French autumn, so slow, so golden, and so melancholy, had begun. At the end of the mighty vista of the Champs Élysées, the Arc de Triomphe rose, brown and vaporous in the exhalations of the quiet city, and an aeroplane was maneuvering over the Place de la Concorde, a moving speck of white and silver in the soft, September blue.

Henry Sheahan, 1915. Courtesy of George J. Mitchell Department of Special Collections & Archives, Bowdoin College Library, Brunswick, Maine.

From a nearby Punch and Judy show the laughter of little children floated down the garden in outbursts of treble shrillness. "Villain, monster, scoundrel," squeaked a voice. Flopped across the base of the stage, the arms hanging downwards, was a prostrate doll which a fine manikin in a Zouave's uniform [bright red cap, blue jacket, and baggy trousers, adopted by French infantry in Algeria in the 1830s] belabored with a stick; suddenly it stirred, and, with a comic effect, lifted its puzzled, wooden head to the laughing children. Beneath a little Prussian helmet was the head of [Kaiser] William of Germany, caricatured with Parisian skill into a scowling, green fellow with a monster black mustache turned up to his eyes. "Lie down!" cried the Zouave doll imperiously. "Here is a love pat for thee from a French Zouave, my big Boche." [*Boche*, from *caboche*, French slang for an obstinate person, was what the French called the Germans.] And he struck him down again with his staff.

Soldiers walked in the garden, permissionnaires (men on furlough) out for an airing with their rejoicing families, smart young English subalterns, and rosy-fleshed, golden-haired Flemings of the type that Rubens drew. But neither their presence nor the sight of an occasional mutilé (soldier who has lost a limb), pathetically clumsy on his new crutches, quite sent home the presence of the war. The normal life of the city was powerful enough to engulf the disturbance, the theaters were open, there were the same crowds on the boulevards, and the same gossipy spectators in the sidewalk cafés. After a year of war the Parisians were accustomed to soldiers, cripples, and people in mourning. The strongest effect of the war was more subtle of definition, it was a change in the temper of the city. Since the outbreak of the war, the sham Paris that was "Gay Paree" had disappeared, and the real Paris, the Paris of tragic memories and great men, had taken its place. Yet in this great, calm city, with its vaporous browns and slatey blues, and its characteristic acrid smell of gasoline fumes, was another Paris, a terrible Paris, which I was that night to see. Early in the afternoon a dull haze of leaden clouds rose in the southwest. It began to rain.[2]

While rain fell on Paris from the west, artillery shells were falling in the east. French and German armies were fighting in the wine province of Champagne. There were heavy casualties on both sides. Henry Sheahan, assigned to the Paris Ambulance Section, was about to have his first call to duty that night.

In a great garret of the hospital, under a high French roof, was the dormitory of the volunteers attached to the Paris Ambulance Section. At night, this great space was lit by only one light, a battered electric reading-lamp standing on a kind of laboratory table in the center of the floor, and window curtains of dark-blue cambric, waving mysteriously in the night wind, were supposed to hide even this glimmer from the eyes of raiding Zeppelins [German dirigibles, or gas-powered airships]. Looking down, early in the evening, into the great quadrangle of the institution, one saw the windows of the opposite wing veiled with this mysterious blue, and heard all the feverish unrest of a hospital, the steps on the tiled corridors, the running of water in the bathroom taps, the hard clatter of surgical vessels, and sometimes the cry of a patient having a painful wound dressed. But late at night the confused murmur of the battle between life and death had subsided, the lights in the wards were extinguished, and only the candle of the night nurse, seen behind a screen, and the stertorous breathing of the many sleepers, brought back the consciousness of human life.

It was late at night, and I stood looking out of my window over the roofs of Neuilly to the great, darkened city just beyond. From somewhere along the tracks of the "Little Belt" railway came a series of piercing shrieks from a locomotive whistle. It was raining hard, drumming on the slate roof of the dormitory, and somewhere below a gutter gurgled foolishly. Far away in the corridor a gleam of yellow light shone from the open door of an isolation room where a nurse was watching by a patient dying of gangrene. Two comrades who had been to the movies at the Gaumont Palace near the Place Clichy began to talk in sibilant whispers of the evening's entertainment, and one of them said, "That war film was a corker; did you spot the big cuss throwing the grenades?" "Yuh, damn good," answered the other pulling his shirt over his head. It was a strange crew that inhabited these quarters; there were idealists, dreamers, men out of work, simple rascals and adventurers of all kinds. To my right slept a big, young Westerner, from some totally unknown college in Idaho, who was a humanitarian enthusiast to the point of imbecility, and to the left a middle-aged rogue who indulged in secret debauches of alcohol and water he cajoled from the hospital orderlies. Yet this obscure and motley community was America's contribution to France. I fell asleep.

"Up, birds!"

The lieutenant of the Paris Section, a mining engineer with a picturesque vocabulary of Nevadan profanity, was standing in his pajama trousers at the head of the room, holding a lantern in his hand.

"Up, birds!" he called again. "Call's come in for Lah Chapelle." There were uneasy movements under the blankets, inmates of adjoining beds began to talk to each other, and some lit their bedside candles. The chief went down both sides of the dormitory, flashing his lantern before each bed, ragging the sleepy. "Get up, So-and-So. Well, I must say, Pete, you have a hell of a nerve." There were glimpses of candle flames, bare bodies shivering in the damp cold, and men sitting on beds, winding on their puttees [cloth strips wrapped around the lower leg: in World War I they were worn to keep mud and water out of boots].

"Gee! listen to it rain," said somebody. "What time is it?" "Twenty minutes past two." Soon the humming and drumming of the motors in the yard sounded through the roaring of the downpour.

Down in the yard I found Oiler, my orderly, and our little Ford ambulance, number fifty-three. One electric light, of that sickly yellow color universal in France, was burning over the principal entrance to the hospital, just giving us light enough to see our way out of the gates. Down the narrow, dark Boulevard Inkerman we turned, and then out on to a great street which led into the "outer" Boulevard des Batignolles and Clichy. To that darkness with which the city, in fear of raiding aircraft, has hidden itself, was added the continuous, pouring rain. In the light of our lamps, the wet, golden trees of the black, silent boulevards shone strangely, and the illuminated advertising kiosks, which we passed, one after the other at the corners of great streets, stood lonely and drenched, in the swift, white touch of our radiance. Black and shiny, the asphalt roadway appeared to go on in a straight line forever and forever.

Neither in residential, suburban Neuilly nor in deserted Montmartre was there a light to be seen, but when we drew into the working quarter of La Chapelle, lights appeared in the windows, as if some toiler of the night was expected home or starting for his labor, and vague forms, battling with the rain or in refuge under the awning of a café, were now and then visible. From the end of the great, mean rue de La Chapelle the sounds of the unrest of the railroad yards began to be heard, for this street leads to the freight-houses near the fortifications. Our objective was a great freight station which the Government, some months before, had turned into a receiving-post for the wounded; it lay on the edge of the yard, some distance in from the street, behind a huddle of smaller sheds and outbuildings. To our surprise the rue de La Chapelle was strewn with ambulances rushing from the station, and along two sides of the great yard, where the merchandise trucks had formerly turned in, six or seven hundred more ambulances were waiting. We turned out of the dark, rain-swept city into this hurly-burly of shouts, snorting of engines, clashing of gears, and whining of brakes, illuminated with a thousand intermeshing beams of headlights across whose brilliance the rain fell in sloping, liquid rods.

"Quick, a small car this way!" cried someone in an authoritative tone, and number fifty-three ran up an inclined plane into the enormous shed which had been reserved for the loading of the wounded into the ambulances.

We entered a great, high, white-washed, warehouse kind of place, about four hundred feet long by four hundred feet wide, built of wood evidently years before. In the middle of this shed was an open space, and along the walls were rows of ambulances. Brancardiers (stretcher-bearers; from brancard, a stretcher) were loading wounded into these cars, and as soon as one car was filled, it would go out of the hall and another would take its place. There was an infernal din; the place smelled like a stuffy garage, and was full of blue gasoline fumes; and across this hurly-burly, which was increasing every minute, were carried the wounded, often nothing but human bundles of dirty blue cloth and fouled bandages. Every one of these wounded soldiers was saturated with mud, a gray-white mud that clung moistly to their overcoats, or, fully dry, colored every part of the uniform with its powder. One saw men that appeared to have rolled over and over in a puddle bath of this whitish mud, and sometimes there was seen a sinister mixture of blood and mire. There is nothing romantic about a wounded soldier, for his condition brings a special emphasis on our human relation to ordinary meat. Dirty, exhausted, unshaven, smelling of the trenches, of his wounds, and of the antiseptics on his wounds, the soldier comes from the train a sight for which only the great heart of Francis of Assisi could have adequate pity.

Oiler and I went through an opening in a canvas partition into that part of the great shed where the wounded were being unloaded from the trains. In width, this part measured four hundred feet, but in length it ran to eight hundred. In two rows of six each, separated by an aisle about eight feet wide, were twelve little houses, about forty feet square, built of stucco, each one painted a different color. The woodwork of the exterior was displayed through the plaster in the Elizabethan fashion, and the little sheds were clean, solidly built, and solidly roofed. In one of these constructions was the bureau of the staff which assigned the wounded to the hospitals, in another was a fully equipped operating-room, and in the others, rows of stretcher-horses, twenty-five to a side, on which the wounded were laid until a hospital number had been assigned them. A slip, with these hospital numbers on it, the names of the patients, and the color of the little house in which they were to be found, was then given to the chauffeur of an ambulance, who, with this slip in hand and followed by a number of stretcher-bearers, immediately gathered his patients. A specimen slip might run thus—"To Hospital 32, avenue de l'Iéna, Paul Chaubard, red barraque, Jules Adamy, green barraque, and Alphonse Fort, ochre barraque."

To give a French touch to the scene, this great space, rapidly filling with human beings in an appalling state of misery, as the aftermath of the offensive broke on us, was decorated with evergreen trees and shrubs so that the effect was that of an indoor fair or exhibition; you felt as if you might get samples of something at each barraque, as the French termed the little houses. To the side of these there was a platform, and a sunken track running along the wall, and behind, a great open space set with benches for those of the wounded able to walk. Some fifty great, cylindrical braziers, which added a strange bit of rosy, fiery color to the scene, warmed this space. When the wounded had begun to arrive at about midnight, a regiment of Zouaves was at hand to help the regular stretcher-bearers; these Zouaves were all young, "husky" men dressed in the baggy red trousers and short blue jacket of their classic uniform, and their strength was in as much of a contrast to the weakness of those whom they handled as their gay uniform was in contrast to the miry, horizon blue of the combatants. There was something grotesque in seeing two of these powerful fellows carrying to the wagons a dirty blue bundle of a human being.

With a piercing shriek, that cut like a gash through the uproar of the ambulance engines, a sanitary train, the seventh since midnight, came into the station, and so smoothly did it run by, its floors on a level with the main floor, that it seemed an illusion, like a stage train. On the platform stood some Zouaves waiting to unload the passengers, while others cleared the barraques and helped the feeble to the ambulances. There was a steady line of stretchers going out, yet the station was so full that hardly a bit of the vast floor space was unoccupied. One walked down a narrow path between a sea of bandaged bodies. Shouldering what baggage they had, those able to walk plodded in a strange, slow tempo to the waiting automobiles. All by themselves were about a hundred poor, ragged Germans, wounded prisoners, brothers of the French in this terrible fraternity of pain.

About four or five hundred assis (those able to sit up) were waiting on benches at the end of the hall. Huddled round the rosy, flickering braziers, they sat profoundly silent in the storm and din that moved about them, rarely conversing with each other. I imagine that the stupefaction, which is the physiological reaction of an intense emotional and muscular effort, had not yet worn away. There were fine heads here and there. Forgetful of his shattered arm, an old fellow, with the face of Henri Quatre [king of France, 1589–1610] eagle nose, beard, and all, sat with his head sunken on his chest in mournful contemplation, and a fine-looking, black-haired, dragoon kind of youth with the wildest of eyes clung like grim death to a German helmet. The same expression of resigned fatalism was common to all.

Sometimes the chauffeurs who were waiting for their clients got a chance to talk to one of the soldiers. Eager for news, they clustered round the wounded man, bombarding him with questions.

"Are the Boches retreating?"

"When did it begin?"

"Just where is the attack located?"

"Are things going well for us?"

The soldier, a big young fellow with a tanned face, somewhat pale from the shock of a ripped-up forearm, answered the questions good-naturedly, though the struggle had been on so great a scale that he could only tell about his own hundred feet of trench. Indeed the substance of his information was that there had been a terrible bombardment of the German lines, and then an attack by the French which was still in progress.

"Are we going to break clear through the lines?"

The soldier shrugged his shoulders. "They hope to," he replied (23–28).

This was the beginning of the Second Battle of Champagne, in the wine country now laced with trenches, from September 25 to October 6. It had begun with a three-day French artillery attack and some French gains afterward, but the German forces retaliated and erased most of the gains. When it was over, the combined French and British casualties totaled 250,000; the Germans lost 72,000.[3]

Just beyond us, in one of the thousand stretchers on the floor, a small bearded man had died. With his left leg and groin swathed in bandages, he lay flat on his back, his mouth open, muddy, dirty, and dead. From time to time the living on each side stole curious, timid glances at him. Then, suddenly, someone noticed the body, and two stretcher-bearers carried it away, and two more brought a living man there in its place.

The turmoil continued to increase. At least a thousand motor-ambulances, mobilized from all over the region of Paris, were now on hand to carry away the human wreckage of the great offensive. Ignorant of the ghastly army at its doors, Paris slept. The rain continued to fall heavily.

"Eh la, comrade." A soldier in his late thirties, with a pale, refined face, hailed me from his stretcher. "You speak French?"

I nodded.

"I am going to ask you to do me a favor—write to my wife who is here in Paris, and tell her that I am safe and shall let her know at once what hospital I am sent to. I shall be very grateful." He let his shoulders sink to the stretcher again and I saw him now and then looking for me in the crowd. Catching my eye, he smiled.

A train full of Algerian troops came puffing into the station, the uproar hardly rising above the general hubbub. The passengers who were able to walk got out first, some limping, some walking firmly with a splendid Eastern dignity. These men were Arabs and Moors from Algeria and Tunisia, who had enlisted in the colonial armies. There was a great diversity of size and racial type among them, some being splendid, big men of the type one imagines Othello to have been, some chunkier and more bullet-headed, and others tall and lean with interesting aquiline features. I fancy that the shorter, rounder-skulled ones were those with a dash of black blood. The uniform, of khaki-colored woolen, consisted of a simple, short-waisted jacket, big baggy trousers, puttees, and a red fez or a steel helmet with the lunar crescent and "R.F." [République Française] for its device. We heard rumors about their having attacked a village. Advancing in the same curious tempo as the French, they passed to the braziers and the wooden benches. Last of all from the train, holding his bandaged arm against his chest, a native corporal with the features of a desert tribesman advanced with superb, unconscious stateliness. As the Algerians sat round the braziers, their uniforms and brown skins presented a contrast to the pallor of the French in their bedraggled blue, but there was a marked similarity of facial expression.

My first assignment, two Algerians and two Frenchmen, took me to an ancient Catholic high school which had just been improvised into a hospital for the Oriental troops. It lay, dirty, lonely, and grim, just to one side of a great street on the edge of Paris, and had not been occupied since its seizure by the State. Turning in through an enormous door, lit by a gas globe flaring and flickering in the torrents of rain, we found ourselves in an enormous, dark courtyard, where a half-dozen ambulances were already waiting to discharge their clients. Along one wall there was a flight of steps, and from somewhere beyond the door at the end of this stair shone the faintest glow of yellow light.

It came from the door of a long-disused schoolroom, now turned into the receiving-hall of this strange hospital. The big, high room was lit by one light only, a kerosene hand lamp standing on the teacher's desk, and so smoked was the chimney that the wick gave hardly more light than a candle. There was just enough illumination to see about thirty Algerians sitting at the school desks, their big bodies crammed into the little seats, and to distinguish others lying in stretchers here and there upon the floor. At the teacher's table a little French adjutant with a trim, black mustache and a soldier interpreter were trying to discover the identity of their visitors.

"Number 2215 (numéro deux mille deux cent quinze), the officer cried; and the interpreter, leaning over the adjutant's shoulder to read the name, shouted, "Méhémet Ali."

There was no answer, and the Algerians looked round at each other, for all the world like children in a school. It was very curious to see these dark, heavy, wild faces bent over these disused desks.

"Number 2168 (numéro deux mille cent soixante huit), cried the adjutant.

"Abdullah Taleb," cried the interpreter.

"Moi," answered a voice from a stretcher in the shadows of the floor.

"Take him to room six," said the adjutant, indicating the speaker to a pair of stretcher-bearers. In the quieter pauses the rain was heard beating on the panes.

There are certain streets in Paris, equally unknown to tour-
ist and Parisian—obscure, narrow, cobble-stoned lanes, lined
by walls concealing little orchards and gardens. So provincial is
their atmosphere that it would be the easiest thing in the world
to believe one's self on the fringe of an old town, just where
little bourgeois villas begin to overlook the fields; but to consider one's self just beyond the heart of Paris is almost incredible. Down such a street, in a great garden, lay the institution to
which our two Frenchmen were assigned. We had a hard time
finding it in the night and rain, but at length, discovering the
concierge's bell, we sent a vigorous peal clanging through the
darkness. Oiler lifted the canvas flap of the ambulance to see
about our patients.

"All right in there, boys?"

"Yes," answered a voice.

"Not cold?"

"Non. Are we at the hospital?"

"Yes; we are trying to wake up the concierge."

There was a sound of a key in a lock, and a small, dark woman opened the door. She was somewhat spinstery in type, her
thin, black hair was neatly parted in the middle, and her face
was shrewd, but not unkindly.

"Deux blessés (two wounded), madame," said I. The woman
pulled a wire loop inside the door, and a far-off bell tinkled.

"Come in," she said. "The porter will be here immediately."
We stepped into a little room with a kind of English look to it,
and a carbon print of the Sistine Madonna on the wall.

"Are they seriously wounded?" she asked.

"I cannot say."

A sound of shuffling, slippered feet was heard, and the porter,
a small, beefy, gray-haired man in his fifties, wearing a pair of
rubber boots, and a rain-coat over a woolen night-dress, came
into the room.

"Two wounded have arrived," said the lady. "You are to help
these messieurs get out the stretchers." The porter looked out of
the door at the taillight of the ambulance, glowing red behind its
curtain of rain.

"Mon Dieu, what a deluge!" he exclaimed, and followed us
forth. With an "Easy there," and "Lift now," we soon had both

of our clients out of the ambulance and indoors. They lay on the floor of the odd, stiff, little room, strange intruders of its primness; the first, a big, heavy, stolid, young peasant with enormous, flat feet, and the second a small, nervous, city lad, with his hair in a bang and bright, uneasy eyes. The mud-stained blue of the uniforms seemed very strange, indeed, beside the Victorian furniture upholstered in worn, cherry-red plush. A middle-aged servant—a big-boned, docile-looking kind of creature, probably the porter's wife—entered, followed by two other women, the last two wearing the same cut of prim black waist and skirt, and the same pattern of white wristlets and collar. We then carried the two soldiers upstairs to a back room, where the old servant had filled a kind of enamel dishpan with soapy water. Very gently and deftly the beefy old porter and his wife took off the fouled, blood-stained uniforms of the two fighting men, and washed their bodies, while she who had opened the door stood by and superintended all. The feverish, bright-eyed fellow seemed to be getting weaker, but the big peasant conversed with the old woman in a low, steady tone, and told her that there had been a big action.

When Oiler and I came downstairs, two little glasses of sherry and a plate of biscuits were hospitably waiting for us. There was something distinctly English in the atmosphere of the room and in the demeanor of the two prim ladies who stood by. It roused my curiosity. Finally one of them said:

"Are you English, gentlemen?"

"No," we replied; "Americans."

"I thought you might be English," she replied in that language, which she spoke very clearly and fluently. "Both of us have been many years in England. We are French Protestant deaconesses, and this is our home. It is not a hospital. But when the call for more accommodations for the wounded came in, we got ready our two best rooms. The soldiers upstairs are our first visitors."

The old porter came uneasily down the stair. "Mademoiselle Pierre says that the doctor must come at once," he murmured, "the little fellow (le petit) is not doing well."

We thanked the ladies gratefully for the refreshment, for we were cold and soaked to the skin. Then we went out again to the ambulance and the rain. A faint pallor of dawn was just beginning. Later in the morning, I saw a copy of the "Matin" attached to a kiosk; it said something about "Grande Victoire."

Thus did the great offensive in Champagne come to the city of Paris, bringing twenty thousand men a day to the station of La Chapelle. For three days and nights the Americans and all the other ambulance squads drove continuously. It was a terrible phase of the conflict to see, but he who neither sees nor understands it cannot realize the soul of the war. . . .

The time was coming when I was to see the mysterious region whence came the wounded of La Chapelle, and, a militaire myself, share the life of the French soldier. Late one evening in October, I arrived in Nancy (28–32).

Henry Sheahan was now a volunteer *poilu*, which means "hairy" or "tough." That was what the French called their soldiers. Ambulance-driver Sheahan found himself in a city about eighteen miles from the line of trenches known as the Western Front. He did his best to describe it.

The day on which I was to go across the great swathe of the front to the first-line trenches dawned cool and sunny. I use the word "swathe" purposely, for only by that image can the real meaning of the phrase "the front" be understood. The thick, black line which figures on the war-maps is a great swathe of country running, with a thousand little turns and twists that do not interfere with its general regularity, from the summits of the Vosges [mountains in northeastern France] to the yellow dunes of the North Sea. The relation of the border of this swathe to the world beyond is the relation of sea to land along an irregular and indented coast. Here an isolated, strategic point, fiercely defended by the Germans, has extended the border of the swathe beyond the usual limits, and villages thirteen and fourteen miles from the actual lines have been pounded to pieces by long-range artillery in the hope of destroying the enemy's communications; there the trenches cross an obscure, level moor upon whose possession nothing particular depends, and the swathe narrows to the villages close by the lines. This swathe, which begins with the French communications, passes the French trenches, leaps "No Man's Land," and continues beyond the German trenches to the German communications, averages about twenty-two miles in width. The territory within this swathe is inhabited by soldiers, ruled by soldiers, worked by soldiers, and organized for war. . . .

Imagine, then, the French half of the swathe extending from the edge of the civilian world to the barbed-wire entanglements of No Man's Land. Within this territory, in the trenches, in the artillery positions, in the villages where troops are quartered (and they are quartered in every village of the swathe), and along all the principal turns and corners of the roads, a certain number of shells fall every twenty-four hours, the number of shells per locality increasing as one advances toward the first lines. . . .

The lieutenant of the American Section, a young Frenchman who spoke English not only fluently, but also with distinction, came to Nancy to take me to the front. It was a clear, sunny morning, and the rumble of the commercial life of Nancy, somewhat later in starting than our own, was just beginning to be heard. Across the street from the breakfast-room of the hotel, a young woman wearing a little black cape over her shoulders rolled up the corrugated iron shutter of a confectioner's shop and began to set the window with the popular patriotic candy boxes, aluminum models of a "seventy-five" shell [a shell seventy-five millimeters in diameter, about nine inches long][4] tied round with a bow of narrow tricolor ribbon; a baker's boy in a white apron and blue jumpers went by carrying a basket of bread on his head; and from the nearby tobacconist's, a spruce young lieutenant dressed in a black uniform emerged lighting a cigarette. At nine in the morning I was contemplating a side street of busy, orderly, sunlit Nancy; that night I was in a cellar seeking refuge from fire shells (33–35).

Beyond the bridge running almost directly north to Metz, lay the historic valley of the Moselle. Great, bare hills, varying between seven hundred and a thousand feet in height, and often carved by erosion into strange, high triangles and abrupt mesas, formed the valley wall. . . . Here and there, on the meadows of the river and the steep flanks of the hills, were ancient, red-roofed villages. . . . But it was at B—, sixteen kilomètres [about ten miles] from Nancy, and sixteen from the lines, that I first felt the imminence of the war. . . .

B— was distinctly a village of the soldiery. The little hamlet, now the junction where the wagon-trains supplying the soldiery meet the great artery of the railroad, was built on the banks of a canal above the river. . . . There were no combatants in it when we passed through, only the old poilus who drove the wagons to the trenches and the army hostlers who looked after the animals. There were pictures of soldier grooms leading horses down a narrow, slimy street between brown, mud-spattered walls to a drinking-trough; of horses lined up along a house wall being briskly curry-combed by big, thick-set fellows in blousy white overalls and blue fatigue caps; and of doors of stables opening on the road showing a bedding of brown straw on the earthen floor. There was a certain stench, too, the smell of horse-fouled mud that mixed with that odor I later was able to classify as the smell of war. For the war has a smell that clings to everything military, fills the troop-trains, hospitals, and cantonments, and saturates one's own clothing, a smell compounded of horse, chemicals, sweat, mud, dirt, and human beings. At the guarded exit of the village to the shell zone was a little military cemetery in which rows of wooden crosses stood with the regularity of pins in a paper.

Two kilomètres [1.24 miles] farther on, at Dieulouard, we drew into the shell zone. A cottage had been struck the day before, and the shell, arriving by the façade of the house, to the left of a door hanging crazily on its hinges, an irregular oval hole, large enough to drive a motor-car through, rose from the ground and came to a point just below the overhang of the roof. The edges of the broken stone were clean and new in contrast to the time-soiled outer wall of the dwelling. A pile of this clean stone lay on the ground at the outer opening of the orifice, mixed with fragments of red tiles.

"They killed two there yesterday," said the lieutenant, pointing out the débris.

The village, a farming hamlet transformed by the vicinity of a great foundry into something neither a village nor a town, was full of soldiers; there were soldiers in the streets, soldiers standing in doorways, soldiers cooking over wood fires, soldiers everywhere. And looking at the muddy village-town full of men in uniforms of blue, old uniforms of blue, muddy uniforms of blue, in blue that was blue-gray and blue-green from wear and exposure to the weather, I realized that the old days of beautiful, half-barbaric uniforms were gone forever, and that, in place of the old romantic war of cavalry charges and great battles in the open, a new, more terrible war had been created, a war that had not the chivalric externals of the old.

After Dieulouard began the swathe of stillness. Following the western bank of the canal of the Moselle the road made a great curve round the base of a hill descending to the river, and then mounted a little spur of the valley wall. Beyond the spur the road went through lonely fields, in which were deserted farmhouses surrounded by acres of neglected vines, now rank and Medusa-like in their weedy profusion. Every once in a while, along a rise, stood great burlap screens so arranged one behind the other as to give the effect of a continuous line when seen from a certain angle.

"What are those for?"

"To hide the road from the Germans. Do you see that little village down there on the crest? The Boches have an observatory there, and shell the road whenever they see anything worth shelling."

A strange stillness pervaded the air; not a stillness of death and decay, but the stillness of life that listens. The sun continued to shine on the brown moorland hills across the gray-green river, the world was quite the same, yet one sensed that something had changed. A village lay ahead of us, disfigured by random shells and half deserted. Beyond the still, shell-spattered houses, a great wood rose, about a mile and a half away, on a ridge that stood boldly against the sky. Running from the edge of the trees down across an open slope to the river was a brownish line that stood in a little contrast to the yellower grass. Suddenly, there slowly rose from this line a great puff of grayish-black smoke which melted away in the clear, autumnal air.

"See," said our lieutenant calmly, with no more emotion than he would have shown at a bonfire—"those are the German trenches. We have just fired a shell into them."

Two minutes more took us into the dead, deserted city of Pont-à-Mousson.

The road was now everywhere screened carefully with lengths of light-brown burlap, and there was not a single house that did not bear witness to the power of a shell. The sense of "the front" began to possess me, never to go, the sense of being in the vicinity of a tremendous power. A ruined village, or a deserted town actually on the front does not bring to mind any impression of decay, for the intellect tends rather to consider the means by which the destruction has been accomplished. One sees villages of the swathes so completely blown to pieces that they are literally nothing but earthy mounds of rubbish, and seeing them thus, in a plain still fiercely disputed night and day between one's own side and the invisible enemy, the mind feels itself in the presence of force, titanic, secret, and hostile.

Beyond Pont-à-Mousson the road led directly to the trenches of the Bois-le-Prêtre, less than half a mile away. But the disputed trenches were hidden behind the trees, and I could not see them. Through the silence of the deserted town sounded the muffled boom of shells and trench engines bursting in the wood beyond, and every now and then clouds of gray-black smoke from the explosion would rise above the brown leaves of the ash trees. The smoke of these explosions rose straight upwards in a foggy column, such as a locomotive might make if, halted on its tracks somewhere in the wood, it had put coal on its fires (36–39).

With the next day I began my service at the trenches, but the war began for me that very night.

A room in a bourgeois flat on the third floor of a deserted apartment house had been assigned me. It was nine o'clock, and I was getting ready to roll up in my blankets and go to sleep. Beneath the starlit heavens the street below was black as pitch save when a trench light, floating serenely down the sky, illuminated with its green-white glow the curving road and the line of dark, abandoned, half-ruinous villas. There was not a sound to be heard outside of an occasional rifle shot in the trenches, sounding for all the world like the click of giant croquet balls. I went round to the rear of the house and looked out of the kitchen windows to the lines. A little action, some quarrel of sentries, perhaps, was going on behind the trees, just where the wooded ridge sloped to the river. Trench light after trench light rose, showing the disused railroad track running across the unharvested fields. Gleaming palely through the French window at which I was standing, the radiance revealed the deserted kitchen, the rusty stove, the dusty pans, and the tarnished water-tap above the stone sink. The hard, wooden crash of grenades broke upon my ears.

My own room was lit by the yellow flame of a solitary candle, rising, untroubled by the slightest breath of wind, straight into the air. . . .

There came a knock at the door, and so still was the town and the house that the knock had the effect of something dramatic and portentous. A big man, with bulging, pink cheeks, a large, chestnut mustache, and brown eyes full of philosophic curiosity, stood in the doorway. The uniform that he was wearing was un-usually neat and clean.

"So you are the American I am to have as neighbor," said he.

"Yes," I replied.

"I am the caporal in charge of the dépôt of the engineers in the cellar," continued my visitor, "and I thought I'd come in and see how you were."

I invited him to enter. . . .

"Well, what do you think of this big racket (ce grand fracas)?"

"I have not seen enough of it to say."

"Well, I think you are going to get a taste of it to-night. I heard our artillery men (nos artiflots) early this morning firing their long-range cannon, and every time they do that the Boch-es throw shells into Pont-à-Mousson. I have been expecting an answer all day. If they start in tonight, get up and come down cellar, son. This house was struck by a shell two weeks ago."

The shadowy, candlelit room and the dark city became at his words more mysterious and hostile. The atmosphere seemed pervaded by some obscure, endless, dreadful threat. It was get-ting toward ten o'clock. . . .

"Don't forget to hurry to the cellar, son," he called as he went away. At his departure the lonely night closed in on me again. Far, far away sounded the booming of cannon.

I am a light sleeper, and the arrival of the first shell awakened me. Kicking off my blankets, I sat up in bed just in time to catch the swift ebb of a heavy concussion. A piece of glass, dislodged from a broken pane by the tremor, fell in a treble tinkle to the floor. For a minute or two there was a full, heavy silence, and then several objects rolled down the roof and fell over the gutters into the street. It sounded as if someone had emptied a hodful of coal onto the house-roof from the height of the clouds. Another silence followed. Suddenly it was broken by a swift, complete sound, a heavy boom-roar, and on the heels of this noise came a throbbing, whistling sigh that, at first faint as the sound of ocean on a distant beach, increased with incredible speed to a whistling swish, ending in a HISH of tremendous volume and a roaring, grinding burst. The sound of a great shell is never a pure bang; one hears, rather, the end of the arriving HISH, the explosion, and the tearing disintegration of the thick wall of iron in one grinding hammer-blow of terrific violence. On the heels of this second shell came voices in the dark street, and the rosy glow of fire from somewhere behind. More lumps, fragments of shell that had been shot into the air by the explosion, rained down upon the roof. I got up and went to the kitchen window. A house on one of the silent streets between the city and the lines was on fire, great volumes of smoke were rolling off into the starlit night, and voices were heard all about murmuring in the shadows. I hurried on my clothes and went down to the cellar.

The light of two candles hanging from a shelf in loops of wire revealed a clean, high cellar; a mess of straw was strewn along one wall, and a stack of shovels and picks, some of them wrapped in paper, was banked against the other. In the straw lay three oldish men, fully clad in the dark-blue uniform which in old times had signaled the Engineer Corps; one dozed with his head on his arm, the other two were stretched out flat in the mysterious grossness of sleep. A door from the cellar to a sunken garden was open, and through this opening streamed the intense radiance of the rising fire. At the opening stood three men, my visitor of the evening, a little, wrinkled man with Napoleon III whiskers [a mustache and a small beard below the lower lip, popularized by Napoleon III, emperor of France from 1852 to 1871, and called the "imperial"],[5] and an old, dwarfish fellow with a short neck, a bullet head, and close-clipped hair. Catching sight of me, my earlier visitor said:

"Well, son, you see it is hammering away (ça tape) ce soir." Hearing another shell, he slammed the door, and stepped to the right behind the stone wall of the cellar.

"Very bad," croaked the dwarf. "The Boches are throwing fire shells."

"And they will fire shrapnel at the poor bougres who have to put out the fires," said the little man with the imperial.

"So they will, those knaves," croaked the dwarf in a voice entirely free from any emotion.

"That fire must be down on the Boulevard Ney," said the bearded man.

"There is another beginning just to the right," said my visitor in the tone of one retailing interesting but hardly useful information.

"There will be others," croaked the dwarf, who, leaning against the cellar wall, was trying to roll a cigarette with big, square, fumbling fingers. . . .

A shell burst very near, and a bitter odor of explosives came swirling through the doorway. A fragment of the shell casing struck a window above us, and a large piece of glass fell by the doorway and broke into splinters. The first fire was dying down, but two others were burning briskly. The soldiers waited for the end of the bombardment, as they might have waited for the end of a thunderstorm.

"Tiens—here comes the shrapnel," exclaimed my visitor. And he slammed the door swiftly. A high, clear whistle cleaved the flame-lit sky, and about thirty small shrapnel shells burst beyond us. "They try to prevent any one putting out the fires," he said confidentially. "They get the range from the light of the flames." Another dreadful rafale (volley) of shrapnel, at the rate of ten or fifteen a minute, came speeding from the German lines. [*Rafale* means "a sudden, violent gust of wind, or a burst of rapid artillery fire."]

"Who puts out the fires?"

"The territorials who police and clean up the town. Some of them live two doors below." My neighbor pointed down the garden to a door opening, like our own, on to an area below the level of the street. Suddenly, a gate opening on a back lane swung back, and two soldiers entered, one carrying the feet and the other the shoulders of a third. The body hung clumsily between them like a piece of old sacking.

"Tiens—someone is wounded." My neighbor spoke to the dwarf: "See who it is."

The dwarf plodded off obediently.

"It is Palester," he announced on his return.

"What's the matter with him?"

"He's been killed" (39–45).

The next day Henry Sheahan visited the trenches of the infamous Bois-le-Prêtre.

Beginning at the right bank of the Meuse, a vast plateau of bare, desolate moorland sweeps eastward to the Moselle, and descends to the river in a number of great, wooded ridges perpendicular to the northward-flowing stream. The town of Pont-à-Mousson lies on an apron of meadowland spread between two of these ridges, the ridge of Puvenelle and the ridge of the Bois-le-Prêtre. The latter is the highest of all the spurs of the valley. Rising from the river about half a mile to the north of the city, it ascends swiftly to the level of the plateau, and was seen from our headquarters as a long, wooded ridge blocking the sky-line to the northwest (45).

Three years later, this wooded ridge was still a battleground. In September 1918 American troops, including Mike Hogg and George Wythe, would finally take it from the Germans.

The Bois-le-Prêtre dominated at once the landscape and our minds. Its existence was the one great fact in the lives of some fifty thousand Frenchmen, Germans, and a handful of exiled Americans; it had dominated and ended the lives of the dead;

it would dominate the imagination of the future. Yet, looking across the brown walls and claret roofs of the hamlet of Maid-ières, there was nothing to be seen but a grassy slope, open fields, a reddish ribbon of road, a wreck of a villa burned by a fire shell, and a wood. The autumn had turned the leaves of the trees, seemingly without exception, to a leathery brown, and in almost all lights the trunks of the trees were a cold, purplish slate. Such was the forest which, battle-areas excepted, has cost more lives than any other point along the line. The wood had been contested trench by trench, literally foot by foot. It was at once the key to the Saint-Mihiel salient and the city of Metz.

The Saint-Mihiel salient—"the hernia," as the French call it—begins at the Bois-le-Prêtre. The salient, as dangerous for the Germans as it is troublesome for the French, represents the lim-it of a German offensive directed against Toul in October, 1914. That the French retreated was due to the fact that the plateau was insufficiently protected, many of the regiments having been rushed north to the great battle then raging on the Aisne. . . .

Metz is the heart of the German organization on the western front: the railroad center, the supply station, the troop dépôt. And the fate of Metz itself hangs on the control of the Bois-le-Prêtre. When the Germans, therefore, retired to the trenches af-ter the battles of September and October, 1914, they took to the ground on the heights of the Bois-le-Prêtre, a terrain far enough ahead of Thiaucourt and Metz to preserve these centers from the danger of being shelled. On the crest of the highest ridge along the valley, admirably ambushed in a thick forest, they waited for the coming of the French. And the French came. . . .

A year later the Bois-le-Prêtre (the Priest Wood), with its per-fume of ecclesiastical names that reminds one of the odor of incense in an old church, had become the Bois de la Mort (the Wood of Death) (45–47).

A young English ambulance driver described this forest as it appeared in June 1915 before Sheahan saw it.

We turned to the left and entered the famous Bois le Prêtre where the artillery had not been. Here was an officers' cemetery, a terrible, sad sight,—six hundred officers' graves. Close by were also the graves of eighteen hundred soldiers. The little cemetery was quite impressive on the side of this lovely green hill with the great trees all around and the little plain wood crosses at each grave. As we waited, a broken-down horse appeared with a cart-load of what looked like old clothes, but which was really *des morts*. I had never seen a dead body until that moment. It was a horrible awakening—eight stiff, mangled, armless bodies—all men like ourselves with people loving them somewhere, all gone this way. A grave had been dug two metres [6.5 feet] deep, large enough to hold sixteen. One by one they were lowered into the grave.[6]

Sheahan and about two dozen other ambulance drivers were soon settled in a new headquarters near the Bois-le-Prêtre.

The house in which our bureau was located was once the summer residence of a rich ironmaster who had fled to Paris at the beginning of the war. . . . It stood behind a high wall of iron spikes on the road leading from Maidières to the trenches. . . . Our bureau in the cellar of "Wisteria Villa" was connected directly with the trenches. When a man had been wounded, he was carried to the poste de secours in the rear lines, and it was our duty to go to this trench post and carry the patient to the hospital at the nearest rail-head. . . .

A hundred yards beyond Wisteria Villa, at a certain corner, the principal road to the trenches divided into three branches, and in order to interfere as much as possible with communications, the Germans daily shelled this strategic point. A comrade and I had the curiosity to keep an exact record of a week's shelling. It must be remembered that the corner was screened from the Germans, who fired casually in the hope of hitting something and annoying the French. The cannons shelling the corner were usually "seventy-sevens," the German quick-firing pieces that correspond to the French "seventy-fives."

Monday, ten shells at 6.30, two at 7.10, five at 11.28, twenty at intervals between 2.15 and 2.45, a swift rafale of some sixteen at 4.12, another rafale of twenty at 8, and occasional shells between 9 and midnight.

Tuesday, two big shells at mid-day.

Wednesday, rafales at 9.14, 11, 2.18, 4.30, and 6.20.

Thursday—no shells.

Friday, twelve at intervals between 10.16 and 12.20. Solitary big shell at 1.05. Another big shell at 3. Some fifteen stray shells between 5 and midnight.

Saturday—no shells.

Sunday—About five shells an hour between 4 in the afternoon and midnight.

I give the number of shells falling at this corner as a concrete instance of what was happening at a dozen other points along the road. The fire of the German batteries was as capricious as the play of a search-light; one week, the corner and three or four other points would catch it, the next week the corner and another set of localities. And there were periods, sometimes ten days to two weeks long, when hardly a shell was fired at any road. Then, after a certain sense of security had begun to take form, a rafale would come screaming over, blow a horse and wagon to pieces, and leave one or two blue figures huddled in the mud. But the French replied to each shell and every rafale, in addition to firing at random all the day and a good deal of the night. There was hardly a night that Wisteria Villa did not rock to the sound of French guns fired at 2 and 3 in the morning. But the average day at Pont-à-Mousson was a day of random silences. The war had all the capriciousness of the sea—of uncertain weather. There were hours of calm in the day, during which the desolate silence of the front flooded swiftly over the landscape; there were interruptions of great violence, sometimes desultory, sometimes beginning, in obedience to a human will, at a certain hour. The outbreak would commence with the orderliness of a clock striking, and continue the greater part of the day, rocking the deserted town with its clamor. Hearing it, the soldiers en repos would say, talking of The Wood [the Bois-le-Prêtre], "It sings (ça chante)," or, "It knocks (ça tape) up there to-day." The smoke of the bursting shells hung over The Wood in a darkish, gray-blue fog. But since The Wood had a personality for us, many would say simply, "Listen to The Wood."

The shell expresses one idea—energy. The cylinder of iron,

piercing the air at a terrific speed, sings a song of swift, appalling energy, of which the final explosion is the only fitting culmination. One gets, too, an idea of an unbending volition in the thing. After a certain time at the front the ear learns to distinguish the sound of a big shell from a small shell, and to know roughly whether or not one is in the danger zone. It was a grim jest with us that it took ten days to qualify as a shell expert, and at the end of two weeks all those who qualified attended the funeral of those who had failed. Life at The Wood had an interesting uncertainty.

A quarter of a mile beyond the corner, on the slope of Puvenelle opposite The Wood, stood Montauville, the last habitable village of the region. To the south of it rose the wooded slopes of Puvenelle; to the north, seen across a marshy meadow, were the slope and the ridge of the Bois-le-Prêtre. The dirty, mud-spattered village was caught between the leathery sweeps of two wooded ridges. Three winding roads, tramped into a pie of mire, crossed the grassy slope of The Wood, and disappeared into the trees at the top. Though less than a mile from the first German line, the village, because of its protection from shells by a spur of the Bois-le-Prêtre, was in remarkably good condition; the only building to show conspicuous damage being the church, whose steeple had been twice struck. It was curious to see pigeons flying in and out of the belfry through the shell rents in the roof. Here and there, among the uncultivated fields of those who had fled, were the green fields of someone who had stayed. A woman of seventy still kept open her grocery shop; it was extraordinarily dirty, full of buzzing flies, and smelled of spilled wine.

"Why did you stay?" I asked her.

"Because I did not want to leave the village. Of course my daughter wanted me to come to Dijon. Imagine me in Dijon, I, who have been to Nancy only once! A fine figure I should make in Dijon in my sabots [wooden shoes]!"

"And are you not afraid of the shells?"

"Oh, I should be afraid of them if I ever went out in the street. But I never leave my shop."

And so she stayed, selling the three staples of the French front,

Camembert cheese, Norwegian sardines, and cakes of chocolate. But Montauville was far from safe. It was there that I first saw a man killed. I had been talking to a sentry, a small young fellow of twenty-one or two, with yellow hair and gray-blue eyes full of weariness. He complained of a touch of jaundice, and wished heartily that the whole affaire—meaning the war in general— was finished. He was very anxious to know if the Americans thought the Boches were going to win. Some vague idea of winning the war just to get even with the Boches seemed to be in his mind. I assured him that American opinion was optimistic in regard to the chances of the Allies, and strolled away. Hardly had I gone ten feet, when a "seventy-seven" shell, arriving without warning, went Zip-bang, and, turning to crouch to the wall, I saw the sentry crumple up in the mud. It was as if he were a rubber effigy of a man blown up with air, and someone had suddenly ripped the envelope. His rifle fell from him, and he, bending from the waist, leaned face down into the mud. I was the first to get to him. The young, discontented face was full of the gray street mud, there was mud in the hollows of the eyes, in the mouth, in the fluffy mustache. A chunk of the shell had ripped open the left breast to the heart. Down his sleeve, as down a pipe, flowed a hasty drop, drop, drop of blood that mixed with the mire (47–50). . . .

At Dieulouard I had entered the shell zone; at Pont-à-Mousson, I crossed the borders of the zone of quiet; at Montauville began the last zone—the zone of invisibility and violence. Civilian life ended at the western end of the village street with the abruptness of a man brought face to face with a high wall. Beyond the village a road was seen climbing the grassy slope of Puvenelle, to disappear as it neared the summit of the ridge in a brown wood. It was just an ordinary hill road of Lorraine, but the fact that it was the direct road to the trenches invested this climbing, winding, silent length with extraordinary character. The gate of the zone of violence, every foot of it bore some scar of the war, now trivial, now gigantic—always awesome in the power and volition it revealed. One passed from the sight of a brown puddle, scooped in the surface of the street by an exploding shell, to a view of a magnificent ash tree splintered by some projectile. It is a very rare thing to see a sinister landscape, but this whole road was sinister (51). . . .

Skirting the ravine, now wooded, between Puvenelle and the Bois-le-Prêtre, the road continued westward till it emerged on the high plateau of La Woevre; the last kilomètre being in full view of the Germans entrenched on the ridge across the rapidly narrowing ravine. Along this visible space the trees and bushes by the roadside were matted by shell fire into an inextricable confusion of destruction, and through the wisps and splinters of this ruin was seen the ridge of the Bois-le-Prêtre rapidly attaining the level of the moor. At length the forest of Puvenelle, the ravine, and the Bois-le-Prêtre ended together in a rolling sweep of furzy fields cut off to the west and north by a vast billow of the moor which, like the rim of a saucer, closed the wide horizon. . . .

There was not a soul anywhere in sight; I was surrounded with evidences of terrific violence—the shattered trees, the shell holes in the road, the brown-lipped craters in the earth of the fields, the battered inn; but there was not a sign of the creators of this devastation. A northwest wind blew in great salvos across the mournful, lonely plateau, rippling the furze, and brought to my ears the pounding of shells from behind the rise. When I got to this rim a soldier, a big, blond fellow of the true Gaulois type with drooping yellow mustaches, climbed slowly out of a hole in the ground. The effect was startling. I had arrived at the line where the earth of France completely swallows up the army. This disappearance of life in a decor of intense action is one of the most striking things of the war. All about in the surface of the earth were little, square, sooty holes that served as chimneys, and here and there rectangular, grave-like openings in the soil showing three or four big steps descending to a subterranean hut. Fifty feet away not a sign of human life could be distinguished. Six feet under the ground, framed in the doorway of a hut, a young, black-haired fellow in a dark-brown jersey stood smiling pleasantly up at us; it was he who was to be my guide to the various postes and trenches that I had need to know. He came up to greet me.

"Better bring him down here," growled a voice from somewhere in the earth. "There have been bullets crossing the road all afternoon."

"I am going to show him the Quart-en-Réserve first."

The Quart-en-Réserve (Reserved Quarter) was the section of the Bois-le-Prêtre which, because of its situation on the crest of the great ridge, had been the most fiercely contested. We crept up on the edge of the ridge and looked over. An open, level field some three hundred yards wide swept from the Thiaucourt road to the edges of the Bois-le-Prêtre; across this field ran in the most confused manner a strange pattern of brown lines that disappeared among the stumps and poles of the haggard wood to the east. To the northwest of this plateau, on the road ahead of us, stood a ruined village caught in the torment of the lines. Here and there, in some twenty or thirty places scattered over the scarred plateau, the smoke of trench shells rose in little curling puffs of gray-black that quickly dissolved in the wind.

"The Quart is never quiet," said my guide. "It is now half ours, half theirs."

Close to the ground, a blot of light flashed swifter than a stroke of lightning, and a heavier, thicker smoke rolled away.

"That is one of ours. We are answering their trench shells with an occasional 'one hundred and twenty.'"

"How on earth is it that everybody is not killed?"

"Because the regiment has occupied the Quart so long that we know every foot, every turn, every shelter of it. When we see a trench shell coming, we know just where to go. It is only the newcomers who get killed. Two months past, when a new regiment occupied the Quart during our absence en repos, it lost twenty-five men in one day."

The first trench that I entered was a simple trench about seven feet deep, with no trimmings whatsoever, just such a trench as might have been dug for the accommodation of a large water conduit. We walked on a narrow board walk very slippery with cheesy, red-brown mire. From time to time the hammer crash of a shell sounded uncomfortably near, and bits of dirt and pebbles, dislodged by the concussion, fell from the wall of the passage. The only vista was the curving wall of the long communication trench and the soft sky of Lorraine, lit with the pleasant sunlight of middle afternoon, and islanded with great golden-white cloud masses. My guide and I might have been the last persons left in a world of strange and terrible noises. The boyau (communication trench) began to turn and wind about in the most perplexing manner, and we entered a veritable labyrinth. This extraordinary, baffling complexity is due primarily to the fact that the trenches advance and retreat, rise and fall, in order to take advantage of the opportunities for defense afforded by every change in the topography of the region. I remember one area along the front consisting of two round, grassy hills divided by a small, grassy valley whose floor rose gently to a low ridge connecting the two heights. In this terrain the defensive line began on the first hill as a semicircle edging the grassy slopes presented to the enemy, then retreated, sinking some forty feet, to take advantage of the connecting link of upland at the head of the ravine, and took semicircular form again on the flat, broad summit of the second hill. In the meadows at the base of these hills a brook flowing from the ravine had created a great swamp, somewhat in the shape of a wedge pointing outward from the mouth of the valley. The lines of the enemy, edging this tract of mire, were consequently in the shape of an open V. Thus the military situation at this particular point may be pictorially represented by a salient semicircle, a dash, and another salient semicircle faced by a wide, open V. Imagine such a situation complicated by offensive and counter-offensive, during which the French have seized part of the hills and the German part of the plain, till the whole region is a madman's maze of barbed wire, earthy lines, trenches,—some of them untenable by either side and still full of the dead who fell in the last combat,—shell holes, and fortified craters. Such was something of the situation in that wind-swept plain at the edge of the Bois-le-Prêtre. . . . Two pictures stand out, particularly, the dead on the barbed wire, and the village called "Fey au Rats" at night.

"The next line is the first line. Speak in whispers now, for if the Boches hear us we shall get a shower of hand-grenades."

I turned into a deep, wide trench whose floor had been trodden into a slop of cheesy, brown mire which clung to the big hobnailed boots of the soldiers. Every foot or so along the parapet there was a rifle slit, made by the insertion of a wedge-shaped wooden box into the wall of brownish sandbags, and the sentries stood about six feet apart. The trench had the hushed quiet of a sickroom.

"Do you want to see the Boches? Here; come, put your eye to this rifle slit."

A horizontal tangle of barbed wire lay before me, the shapeless gully of an empty trench, and, thirty-five feet away, another blue-gray tangle of barbed wire and a low ripple of the brownish earth. As I looked, one of the random silences of the front stole swiftly into the air. French trench and German trench were perfectly silent; you could have heard the ticking of a watch.

"You never see them?"

"Only when we attack them or they attack us."

An old poilu, with a friendly smile revealing a jagged reef of yellow teeth, whispered to me amiably:

"See them? Good Lord, it's bad enough to smell them. You ought to thank the good God, young man, that the wind is carrying it over our heads."

"Any wounded to-day?"

"Yes; a corporal had his leg ripped up about half an hour ago."

At a point a mile or so farther down the moor I looked again out of a rifle box. No Man's Land had widened to some three hundred feet of waving furze, over whose surface gusts of wind passed as over the surface of the sea. About fifty feet from the German trenches was a swathe of barbed wire supported on a row of five stout, wooden posts. So thickly was the wire strung that the eye failed to distinguish the individual filaments and saw only the rows of brown-black posts filled with a steely purple mist. Upon this mist hung masses of weather-beaten blue rags whose edges waved in the wind.

"Des camarades" (comrades), said my guide very quietly.

A month later I saw the ruined village of Fey-en-Haye by the light of the full golden shield of the Hunters' [October] Moon. The village had been taken from the Germans in the spring, and was now in the French lines, which crossed the village street and continued right on through the houses. "The first village on the road to Metz" had tumbled, in piles and mounds of rubbish, out on a street grown high with grass. Moonlight poured into the roofless cottages, escaping by shattered and jagged rents, and the mounds of debris took on fantastic outlines and cast strange shadows. In the middle of the village street stood two wooden crosses marking the graves of soldiers. It was the Biblical "Abomination of Desolation."

Looking at Fey from the end of the village street, I slowly realized that it was not without inhabitants. Wandering through the grass, scurrying over the rubbish heaps, running in and out of the rumbling thresholds, were thousands and thousands of rats (52–56).

Fey-en-Haye had once been a quiet little village with one street, a church, and 150 residents.

During the months he spent on duty near the Bois-le-Prêtre, Sheahan found time to think about the enormity of trench warfare.

By a strange decree of fate, a new warfare has come into being, admirably adapted to the use and the testing of all our faculties, organizations, and inventions—trench warfare. The principal element of this modern warfare is lack of mobility. The lines advance, the lines retreat, but never once, since the establishment of the present trench swathe, have the lines of either combatant been pushed clear out of the normal zone of hostilities. The fierce, invisible combats are limited to the first-line positions, averaging a mile each way behind No Man's Land. This stationary character has made the war a daily battle; it has robbed war of all its ancient panoply, its cavalry, its uniforms brilliant as the sun, and has turned it into the national business. I dislike to use the word "business," with its usual atmosphere of orderly bargaining; I intend rather to call up an idea more familiar to American minds— the idea of a great intricate organization with a corporate volition. The war of today is a business, the people are the stockholders, and the object of the organization is the wisest application of violence to the enemy. . . .

The front is divided, according to military exigencies, into a number of roughly equal lengths called secteurs. Each secteur is an administrative unit with its own government and its own system adapted to the local situation. The heart of this unit is the railroad station at which the supplies arrive for the shell zone; in a normal secteur, one military train arrives every day bringing the needed supplies, and one hospital train departs, carrying the sick and wounded to the hospitals. The station at the front is always a scene of considerable activity, especially when the train arrives; there are pictures of old poilus in red trousers pitching out yellow hay for the horses, commissary officers getting their rations, and artilleurs stacking shells. The train not being able to continue into the shell zone, the supplies are carried to the distributing station at the trenches in a convoy of wagons, called the ravitaillement [supply]. Every single night, somewhere along the road, each side tries to smash up the other's ravitaillement. To avoid this, the ravitaillement wagons start at different hours after dark, now at dusk, now at midnight. Sometimes, close by the trenches on a clear, still night, the plashing and creaking of the enemy's wagons can be heard through the massacred trees. I remember being shelled along one bleak stretch of moorland road just after a drenching December rain. The trench lights rising over The Wood, three miles away, made the wet road glow with a tarnished glimmer, and burnished the muddy pools into mirrors of pale light. The ravitaillement creaked along in the darkness. Suddenly a shell fell about a hundred yards away, and the wagons brought up jerkily, the harnesses rattling. For ten minutes the Germans shelled the length of road just ahead of us, but no shell came closer to us than the first one. About thirty "seventy-seven" shells burst, some on the road, some on the edges of the fields; we saw them as flashes of reddish-violet light close to the ground. In the middle of the mêlée a trench light rose, showing the line of halted gray wagons, motionless horses, and the helmeted drivers. The whole affair passed in silence. When it was judged that the last shell had fallen, whips cracked like pistol shots, and the line lumbered on again.

The food came to us fresh every day in a freight car fitted up like a butcher's shop, in charge of a poilu who was a butcher in civilian life.

"So many men—so many grammes," and he would cut you off a slice. There was a daily potato ration, and a daily extra, this last from a list ten articles long which began again every ten days, and included beans, macaroni, lentils, rice, and cheese. The French army is very well and plenteously fed. Coffee, sugar, wine, and even tea are ungrudgingly furnished. These foods are taken directly to the rear of the trenches where the regimental cooks have their traveling kitchens. Once the food is prepared, the cooks—the beloved cuistots—take it to the trenches in great, steaming kettles and distribute it to the men individually. As for clothing, every regiment has a regimental tailor shop and supply of uniforms in the village where they go to repos [a rest area away from the battle lines]. I have often seen the soldier tailor of one of the regiments, a little Alsatian Jew, sewing up the shell rents in a comrade's greatcoat. He had his shop in a pleasant kitchen, and used to sit beside the fire sewing as calmly as an old woman.

The sanitary arrangements of the trenches are the usual army latrines, and very severe punishments are inflicted for any fouling.

If a man is wounded, the medical service man of his squad (infirmier), or one of the stretcher-bearers (brancardiers), takes him as quickly as possible to the regimental medical post in the rear lines. If the trench is getting heavily shelled, and the wound is slight, the attendant takes the man to a shelter and applies first aid until a time comes when he and his patient can proceed to the rear with reasonable safety. At this rear post the regimental surgeon cleans the wound, stops the bleeding, and sends for the ambulance, which, at the Bois-le-Prêtre, came right into the heart of the trenches by sunken roads that were in reality broad trenches. The man is then taken to the hospital that his condition requires, the slightly wounded to one hospital, and those requiring an operation to another. The French surgical hospitals all along the front are marvels of cleanliness and order. The heart of each hospital is the power plant, which sterilizes the water, runs the electric lights, and works the X-ray generator. Mounted on an automobile body, it is always ready to decamp in case the locality gets too dangerous. You find these great, lumbering affairs, half steamroller, half donkey-engine, in the courtyards of old castles, schools, and great private houses close by the front (57–59). . . .

The trench theory is built about the soldier. It must preserve him as far as possible from artillery and from an infantry attack. The defenses begin with barbed wire; then come the rifles and the machine guns; and behind them the light artillery, the "seventy-fives," and the heavy artillery, the "one hundred and twenties," "two hundred and twenties," and, now, an immense howitzer whose real caliber has been carefully concealed. To take a trench position means the crossing of the entanglements of No Man's Land under fire from artillery, rifles, and machine guns, an almost impossible proceeding. An advance is possible only after the opposing trenches have been made untenable by the concentration of artillery fire.

The great offensives begin by blowing the first lines absolutely to pieces; this accomplished, the attacking infantry advances to the vacated trenches under the rifle fire of those few whom the terrible deluge of shells has not killed or crazed, works toward the strong second position under a concentrated artillery fire of the retreating enemy as terrible as its own, fights its way heroically into the second position, and stops there. The great line has been bent, has been dented, but never broken. An offensive must cover at least twenty miles of front, for if the break is too narrow the attacking troops will be massacred by the enemy artillery at both ends of the broken first lines. If the front lines are one mile deep, the artillery must put twenty-five square miles of trenches hors de combat, a task that takes millions of shells. By the time that the first line has been destroyed and the troops have reached the second line, the shells and the men are pretty well used up. A great successful offensive on the western front is theoretically possible, given millions of men, but practically impossible (60–61). . . .

There was one part of the Bois-le-Prêtre region upon which nothing depended, and the war had there settled into the casual exchange of powder and old iron that obtains upon two thirds of the front. At the entrance to this position, in the shadow of a beautiful clump of ash trees, stood the rustic shelters of the regimental cooks. From behind the wall of trees came a terrifying crash. The war-gray, iron field kitchen, which the army slang calls a contre-torpilleur (torpedo-boat destroyer), stood in a little clearing of the wood; there was nothing beautiful to the machine, which was simply an iron box, two feet high and four feet square, mounted on big wheels, and fitted with a high oval chimney. A halo of kitcheny smell floated about it, and the open door of its fire-box, in which brands were burning furiously, and a jet of vapor from somewhere, gave it quite the appearance of an odd steam engine. Beside the contre-torpilleur stood the two cooks. I knew these men very well; one, the older, was a farm-hand in a village of Touraine, and the other, an errand boy in a bookbinding works at Saint-Denis. The war had turned them into regimental cooks, though it was the older man who did most of the cooking (62).

Sheahan continued his description of the Bois-le-Prêtre's trenches.

The road now entered the wood, and continued straight ahead down a pleasant vista of young ash trees. Suddenly a trench, bearing its name in little black, dauby letters on a piece of yellow board the size of a shingle, began by the side of the forest road, and I went down into it as I might have gone down cellar. The Boyau Poincaré—such was its title—began to curve and twist in the manner of trenches, and I came upon a corner in the first line known as "Three Dead Men," because after the capture of the wood, three dead Germans were found there in myste-rious, lifelike attitudes. The names of trenches on the French front often reflect that deep, native instinct to poetry possessed by simple peoples—the instinct that created the English ballads and the exquisite mediaeval French legends of the saints. Other trench names were symbolic, or patriotic, or political; we had the "Trench of the Great Revenge," the "Trench of France," the "Trench of Aristide" (meaning Briand), and the "Boulevard Jof-fre."

Beyond "Les Trois Morts," began the real lines of the posi-tion, and as I wound my way through them to the first lines, the pleasant forest of autumnal branches thinned to a wood of trees bare as telegraph poles. It had taken me half an hour to get from the cook's shelters to the first lines, and during that time I had not heard one single explosion. In the first trench the men stood casually by their posts at the parapet, their bluish coats in an interesting contrast to the brown wall of the trench. Behind the sentries, who peered through the rifle slits every once in a while, flowed the usual populace of the first-line trench, passing as casually as if they were on a Parisian sidewalk, officers as miry as their men, poilus of the Engineer Corps with an eye to the state of the rifle boxes, and an old, unshaven soldier in light-brown corduroy trousers and blue jacket, who volunteered the information that the Boches had thrown a grenade at him as he turned the corner "down there"—

"It didn't go off."

So calm an atmosphere pervaded the cold, sunny, autumnal afternoon that the idea "the trenches" took on the proportions of a gigantic hoax; we might have been masqueraders in the trenches after the war was over. And the Germans were only seventy-five feet away, across those bare poles, stumps, and matted dead brown leaves!

"Attention!" The atmosphere of the trench changed in a second. Every head in sight looked up searchingly at the sky. Just over the trees, distinctly seen, was a little, black, cylindrical package somersaulting through the air. In another second everybody had calculated the spot in which it was about to land, and those whom it threatened had swiftly found shelter, either by continuing down the trench to a sharp turn, running into the door of an abri (shelter), or simply snuggling into a hole dug in the side of the trench. There was a moment of full, complete silence between the time when everybody had taken refuge and the explosion of the trench shell. The missile burst with that loud hammer pound made by a thick-walled iron shell, and lay smoking in the withered leaves.

"It begins—it begins," said an old poilu, tossing his head. "Now we shall have those pellets all afternoon."

An instant after the burst the trench relaxed; some of the sentries looked back to see where the shell had fallen, others paid no attention to it whatsoever. Once again the quiet was disturbed by a muffled boom somewhere ahead of us, and everybody calculated and took refuge exactly as before. The shells began to come, one on the heels of the other with alarming frequency; hardly had one burst when another was discovered in the air. The poilus, who had taken the first shells as a matter of course, good-naturedly even, began to get as cross as peevish schoolboys. It was decidedly too much of a good thing. Finally the order was given for every one except the sentinels, who were standing under the occasional shelters of beams and earth bridged across the trench, to retire to the abris.

The abri to which we retired was about twenty-five feet long and eight feet wide, and had a door at either end. The hut had been dug right in the crude, calcareous rock of Lorraine, and the beams of the roof were deeply set into these natural walls. Along the front wall ran a corridor about a foot wide, and between this corridor and the rear wall was a raised platform about seven feet wide piled with hay. Sprawled in this hay, in various attitudes, were about fifteen men, the squad that had just completed its sentry service. Two candles hung from the massive roof and flickered in the draughts between the two doors, revealing, in rare periods of radiance, a shelf along the wall over the sleepers' heads piled with canteens, knapsacks, and helmets. In the middle of the rock wall by the corridor a semicircular funnel had been carved out to serve as a fireplace, and at its base a flameless fire of beautiful, crumbling red brands was glowing. This hearth cut in the living rock was very wonderful and beautiful. Suddenly a trench shell landed right on the roof of the abri, shaking little fragments of stone down into the fire on the hearth. The soldiers, who sat hunched up on the edge of the platform, their feet in the corridor, gave vent to a burst of anger that had its source in exasperation.

"This is going too far."—"Why don't they answer?"—"Are those dirty cows (the classic sales vaches) going to keep this up all afternoon?" . . .

A shell coming toward you from the enemy makes a good deal of noise, but it is not to be compared to the noise made by one's own shells rushing on a slant just over one's head to break in the enemy's trenches seventy-five feet away. A swift rafale of some fifty "seventy-five" shells passed whistling like the great wind of the Apocalypse, which is to blow when the firmament collapses. Looking through the rifle slit, after the rafale was over, I could see puffs of smoke apparently rising out of the carpet of dead leaves. The . . . sentry held up his finger for us not to make the slightest noise and whispered,—

"I heard somebody yell."

"Where?"

"Over there by that stump."

We strained our ears to catch a sound, but heard nothing.

"I heard the yell plainly," replied the sentry.

The news seemed to give some satisfaction. At any rate, the Germans stopped their trench shells. The quiet hush of late afternoon was at hand. Soon the cook came down the trench with kettles of hot soup (62–66).

One morning, in the little village of Montauville, Sheahan found an unexpected respite from the sounds of war.

The schoolmaster (instituteur) and the schoolmistress (institutrice) of Montauville were a married couple, and had a flat of four rooms on the second story of the schoolhouse. The kitchen of this flat had been struck by a shell, and was still a mess of plaster, bits of stone, and glass, and a fragment had torn clear through the sooty bottom of a copper saucepan still hanging on the wall. In one of the rooms, else quite bare of furniture, was an upright piano. Sometimes while stationed at Montauville, I whiled away the waits between calls to the trenches in playing this instrument.

It was about nine o'clock in the morning, and thus far not a single call had come in. The sun was shining very brightly in a sky washed clear by a night of rain, the morning mists were rising from the wood, and up and down the very muddy street walked little groups of soldiers. I drew up the rickety stool and began to play the waltz from "The Count of Luxembourg." In a short time I heard the sound of tramping on the stairs. In came three poilus—a pale boy with a weary, gentle expression in his rather faded blue eyes; a dark, heavy fellow of twenty-five or six, with big wrists, big, muscular hands, and a rather unpleasant, lowering face; and a little, middle-aged man with straightforward, friendly hazel eyes and a pointed beard. The pale, boyish one carried a violin made from a cigar box under his arm. . . . This violin was very beautifully made, and decorated with a rustic design. I stopped playing.

"Don't, don't," cried the dark, big fellow; "we haven't heard any music for a long time. Please keep on. Jacques, here, will accompany you."

"I never heard the waltz," said the violinist; "but if you play it over for me once or twice, I'll try to get the air—if you would like to have me to," he added with a shy, gentle courtesy.

So I played the rather banal waltz again, till the lad caught the tune. He hit it amazingly well, and his ear was unusually true. The dark one had been in Canada and was hungry for American rag-time. "'The Good Old Summer Time'—you know that? 'Harrigan'—you know that?" he said in English. The rag-time of "Harrigan" floated out on the street of Montauville. But I did not care to play things which could have no violin obligato, so I began to play what I remembered of waltzes dear to every Frenchman's heart—the tunes of the "Merry Widow." "Sylvia" went off with quite a dash. The concert was getting popular. Somebody wanted to send for a certain Alphonse who had an ocarina. Two other poilus, men in the forties, came up, their dark-brown, horseshoe beards making them look like brothers. Side by side against the faded paper on the sunny wall they stood, surveying us contentedly. The violinist, who turned out to be a Norman, played a solo—some music-hall fantasy, I imagine. The next number was the ever popular "Tipperaree," which every single poilu in the French army has learned to sing in a kind of English. Our piano-violin duet hit off this piece even better than the "Merry Widow." I thanked Heaven that I was not called on to translate it, a feat frequently demanded of the American drivers. The song is silly enough in the King's English, but in lucid, exact French, it sinks to positive imbecility.

"You play, don't you?" said the violinist to the small bearded man.

"A little," he replied modestly.

"Please play."

The little man sat down at the piano, meditated a minute, and began to play the rich chords of Rachmaninoff's "Prelude." He got about half through, when Zip-bang! a small shell burst down the street. The dark fellow threw open the French window. The poilus were scurrying to shelter. The pianist continued with the "Prelude."

Zip-bang! Zip-bang! Zshh—Bang—Bang. Bang-Bang!

The piano stopped. Everybody listened. The village was still as death. Suddenly down the street came the rattle of a volley of rifle shots. Over this sound rose the choked, metallic notes of a bugle-call. The rifle shots continued. The ominous popping of machine guns resounded. The village, recovering from its silence, filled with murmurs. Bang! Bang! Bang! Went some more shells. The same knowledge took definite shape in our minds.

"An attack!"

The violinist, clutching his instrument, hurried down the stairs followed by all the others, leaving the chords of the uncompleted "Prelude" to hang in the startled air. Shells were popping everywhere—crashes of smoke and violence—in the roads, in the fields, and overhead. The Germans were trying to isolate the few detachments en repos in the village, and prevent reinforcements from coming in from Dieulouard or any other place. To this end all the roads between Pont-à-Mousson and the trenches and the roads leading directly to the trenches, were being shelled.

"Go at once to Poste C!"

The winding road lay straight ahead, and just at the end of the village street, the Germans had established a tir-de-barrage. This meant that a shell was falling at that particular point about once every fifty seconds. I heard two rafales break there as I was grinding up the machine. Up the slope of Montauville hill came several of the other drivers . . . also evidently bound for Poste C. German bullets, fired wildly from the ridge of The Wood over the French trenches, sang across the Montauville valley, lodging in the trees of the Puvenelle behind us with a vicious *tspt*; shells broke here and there on the stretch leading to the Quart-en-Réserve, throwing small rocks of the road surfacing wildly in every direction. The French batteries to our left were firing at the Germans, the German batteries were firing at the French trenchers and the roads, and the machine guns rattled ceaselessly.

I saw the poilus hurrying up the muddy roads of the slope of the Bois-le-Prêtre—vague masses of moving blue on the brown ways. A storm of shells was breaking round certain points in the road and particularly at the entrance to The Wood. I wondered what had become of the audience at the concert. Various sounds, transit of shells, bursting of shells, crashing of near-by cannon, and rat-tat-tat-tat! of mitrailleuses [machine guns] played the treble to a roar formed of echoes and cadences—the roar of battle. The Wood of Death (Le Bois de la Mort) was singing again (68–70).

We hurried our wounded to the hospital, passing on our way detachments of soldiers rushing toward The Wood from the villages of the region. Three or four big shells had just fallen in Dieulouard, and the village was deserted and horribly still. The wind carried the roar of the attack to our ears. In three quarters of an hour, I was back again at the same moorland poste, to which an order of our commander had attached me. Montauville was full of wounded. I had three on stretchers inside, one beside me on the seat, and two others on the front mudguards. And The Wood continued to sing. From Montauville I could hear the savage yells and cries which accompanied the fighting (71).

In February 1916 Sheahan's ambulance section was ordered to move to the French town of Bar-le-Duc, in preparation for the Battle of Verdun. He reminisced about his time in harm's way in Pont-à-Mousson.

The most interesting question of the whole business is, "How do the soldiers stand it?" At the beginning of my own service, I thought Pont-à-Mousson, with its ruins, its danger, and its darkness, the most awful place on the face of the earth. After a little while, I grew accustomed to the décor, and when the time came for me to leave it, I went with as much regret as if I were leaving the friendliest, most peaceful of towns. First the décor, growing familiar, lost the keener edges of its horror, and then the life of the front—the violence, the destruction, the dying and the dead—all became casual, part of the day's work. A human being is profoundly affected by those about him; thus, when a new soldier finds himself for the first time in a trench, he is sustained by the attitude of the veterans. Violence becomes the commonplace; shells, gases, and flames are the things that life is made of. The war is another lesson in the power of the species to adapt itself to circumstances (72).

Before he left for his new assignment, Sheahan took a solitary walk through Pont-à-Mousson. It had once been a city of 17,000. Now it had a population of about 900.

....

The destroyed quarter of Pont-à-Mousson lay between the main street and the flank of the Bois-le-Prêtre. The quarter was almost totally deserted, probably not more than ten houses being inhabited out of several thousand. The streets that led into it had grass growing high in the gutters, and a velvety moss wearing a winter rustiness grew packed between the paving-stones. Beyond the main street, la rue Fabvrier went straight down this loneliness, and halted or turned at a clump of wrecked houses a quarter of a mile away. Over this clump, slatey-purple and cold, appeared the Bois-le-Prêtre, and every once in a while a puffy cloud of greenish-brown or gray-black would float solemnly over the crests of the trees. This stretch of la rue Fabvrier was one of the most melancholy pictures it was possible to see. Hardly a house had been spared by the German shells; there were pock-marks and pits of shell fragments in the plaster, window glass outside, and holes in walls and roofs. I wandered down the street, passing the famous miraculous statue of the Virgin of Pont-à-Mousson. The image, only a foot or two high and quite devoid of facial expression, managed somehow to express emotion in the outstretched arms, drooping in a gesture at once of invitation and acceptance. A shell had maculated the wall on each side and above the statue, but the little niche and canopy were quite untouched. The heavy sound of my soldier boots went dump! clump! down the silence (79–80). . . .

A melancholy dusk was beginning as I turned home . . . and the deserted streets were filling with purplish shadows. The concussion of exploding shells had blown almost all the glass out of the windows of the Church of St. Laurent, and the few brilliant red and yellow fragments that still clung to the twisted leaden frames reminded me of the autumn leaves that sometimes cling to winter-stricken trees. The interior of the church was swept and garnished, and about twenty candles with golden flames, slowly waving in the drafts from the ruined windows, shone beneath a statue of the Virgin. There was not another soul in the church. A terrible silence fell with the gathering darkness.

In a little wicker basket at the foot of the benignant mother were about twenty photographs of soldiers, some in little brassy frames with spots of verdigris on them, some the old-fashioned "cabinet" kind, some on simple post-cards. There was a young, dark Zouave who stood with his hand on an ugly little table, a sergeant of the Engineer Corps with a vacant, uninteresting face, and two young infantry men, brothers, on the same shabby finger-marked post-card. Pious hands had left them thus in the care of the unhappy mother, "Marie, consolatrice des malheureux [comforter of the sad]."

The darkness of midnight was beginning at Pont-à-Mousson, for the town was always as black as a pit. On my way home I saw a furtive knife edge of yellow light here and there under a door. The sentry stood by his shuttered lantern. Suddenly the first of the trench lights flowered in the sky over the long dark ridge of the Bois-le-Prêtre (82–83).

French soldiers were entitled to periodic escapes from the harrowing world of the Bois-le-Prêtre: There was regular rotation of troops from the frontline trenches to the rear, for a brief *repos*—such as it was.

When the poilus have faced the Boches for two weeks in the trenches, they march down late at night to a village behind the lines, far enough away from the batteries to be out of danger of everything except occasional big shells, and near enough to be rushed up to the front in case of an attack. There they are quartered in houses, barns, sheds, and cellars, in everything that can decently house and shelter a man. These two weeks of repos are the poilus' Elysium, for they mean rest from strain, safety, and comparative comfort. . . .

The village of cantonnement [billeting] is pretty sure to be the usual brown-walled, red-roofed village of Lorraine clumped round its parish church or mouldering castle. In such a French village there is always a hall, usually over the largest wineshop, called the "Salle de Fêtes," and this hall serves for the concert each regiment gives while en repos. The Government provides for, indeed insists upon, a weekly bath, and the bathhouse, usually some converted factory or large shed, receives its daily consignments of companies, marching up to the douches as solemnly as if they were going to church. Round the army continues the often busy life of the village, for to many such a hamlet the presence of a multitude of soldiers is a great economic boon. Grocery shops, in particular, do a rushing business, for any soldier who has a sou is glad to vary the government menu with such delicacies as patés de foie gras, little sugar biscuits, and the well-beloved tablet of chocolate. . . .

Sometimes swish bang! a big shell comes in unexpectedly, and the shopkeepers and clients hurry, at a decent tempo, to the cellar. There, in the earthy obscurity, one sits down on empty herring-boxes and vegetable cases to wait calmly for the exasperating Boches to finish their nonsense. There is a smell of kerosene oil and onions in the air. A lantern, always on hand for just such an emergency, burns in a corner.

"Have you had a bad time in the trenches this week, Monsieur Levarault?" says the épicière [grocer] to a big, stolid soldier who is a regular customer.

"No, quite passable, Madame Champaubert."

"And Monsieur Petticollot, how is he?"

"Very well, thank you, madame. His captain was killed by a rifle grenade last week."

"Oh, the poor man."

Crash goes a shell. Everybody wonders where it has fallen. In a few seconds the éclats [splinters, bursts] rain down into the street.

"Dirty animals," says the voice of the old man in the darkest of all the corners.

The poilus who come to the village en repos are from every part of France, and are of all ages between nineteen and forty-five. I remember seeing a boy aged only fourteen who had enlisted, and was a regular member of an artillery regiment. The average regiment includes men of every class and caste, for every Frenchman who can shoulder a gun is in the war (84–86). . . .

The men who tramp into the village at one and two o'clock in the morning are men who have for two weeks been under a strain that two years of experience has robbed of its intensity.

But strain it is, nevertheless, as the occasional carrying of a ma-
niac reveals. They know very well why they are fighting; even
the most ignorant French laborer has some idea as to what the
affair is all about. The Boches attacked France who was peaceful-
ly minding her own business; it was the duty of all Frenchmen
to defend France, so everybody went to the war. And since the
war has gone on for so long, it must be seen through to the very
end. Not a single poilu wants peace or is ready for peace. And
the French, unlike the English, have continually under their eyes
the spectacle of their devastated land. Yet I heard no ferocious
talk about the Germans, no tales of French cruelty toward German prisoners (87). . . .

The little group to which I was most attached, and for whose
hospitality and friendly greeting I shall always be a debtor, consisted of Belin, a railroad clerk; Bonnefon, a student at the École
des Beaux-Arts; Magne, a village schoolmaster in the Dauphiné;
and Grétry, proprietor of a butcher's shop in the Latin Quarter of
Paris. Belin and Magne had violins which they left in the care of
a café-keeper in the village, and used to play on them just before
dinner. The dinner was served in the house of the village woman
who prepared the food of these four, for sous-officiers are entitled
to eat by themselves if they can find any one kind enough to look
after the cooking. If they can't, then they have to rely entirely on
the substantial but hardly delicious cuisine of their regimental cu-
istot. However, at this village, Madame Brun, the widow of the
local carpenter, had offered to take the popotte, as the French term
an officer's mess. We ate in a room half parlor, half bedchamber,
decorated exclusively with holy pictures. This was a good specimen menu—bread, vermicelli soup, apple fritters, potato salad,
boiled beef, red wine, and coffee. Of this dinner, the Government
furnished the potatoes, the bread, the meat, the coffee, the wine,
and the condiments; private purses paid for the fritters, the vermicelli, and the bits of onion in the salad. Standing round their barns
the private soldiers were having a tasty stew of meat and potatoes
cooked by the field kitchen, bread, and a cupful of boiled lentils
(known in the army as "edible bedbugs"), all washed down with
the army pinard, or red wine (88–89). . . .

Every three months, if the military situation will allow of it and every other man in his group has likewise been away, the French soldier gets a six days' furlough. The slips of paper which are then given out are called feuilles de permission, and the lucky soldier is called a permissionnaire. When the combats that gave the Bois-le-Prêtre its sinister nickname began to peter out, the poilus who had done the fighting were accorded these little vacations, and almost every afternoon the straggling groups of joyous permissionnaires were seen on the road between the trenches and the station. The expression on the faces was never that of having been rescued from a living hell; it expressed joy and prospect of a good time rather than deliverance (93–94).

Times like these were all too few. In the bleak winter of 1916 the Battle of Verdun was about to begin. Sheahan, on a brief turn as a *permissionnaire*, visited Paris and then Lyon, where he had once taught school and where he saw some boys who were now soldiers.

In Lyon I saw a sight at once ludicrous and pathetic. Two little dragoons of the class of 1917, stripling boys of eighteen or nineteen at the most, walked across the public square; their uniforms were too large for them, the skirts of their great blue mantles barely hung above the dust of the street, and their enormous warlike helmets and flowing horse tails were ill-suited to their boyish heads. As I looked at them, I thought of the blue bundles I had seen drying upon the barbed wire, and felt sick at the brutality of the whole awful business. The sun was shining over the bluish mists of Lyon, and the bell of old Saint-Jean was ringing. Two Zouaves, stone blind, went by, guided by a little, fat infirmier [nurse]. At the frontier, the General Staff was preparing for the defense of Verdun.

One great nation, for the sake of a city valueless from a military point of view, was preparing to kill several hundred thousand of its citizens, and another great nation, anxious to retain the city, was preparing calmly for a parallel hecatomb. There is something awful and dreadful about the orderliness of a great offensive, for while one's imagination is grasped by the grandeur and the organization of the thing, all one's faculties of intellect are revolted by the stark brutality of death en masse.

Early in February we were called to Bar-le-Duc, a pleasant old city some distance behind Verdun. Several hundred thousand men were soon going to be killed and wounded, and the city was in a feverish haste of preparation. So many thousand cans of ether, so many thousand pounds of lint, so many million shells, so many ambulances, so many hundred thousand litres of gasoline. Nobody knew when the Germans were going to strike.

During the winter great activity in the German trenches near Verdun had led the French to expect an attack, but it was not till the end of January that aeroplane reconnoitering made certain the imminence of an offensive. As a first step in countering it, the French authorities prepared in the villages surrounding Bar-le-Duc a number of dépôts for troops, army supplies, and ammunition. Of this organization, Bar-le-Duc was the key. The preparations for the counter-attack were there centralized. Day after day convoys of motor-lorries carrying troops ground into town and disappeared to the eastward; big mortars mounted on trucks came rattling over the pavements to go no one knew where; and khaki-clad troops, troupes d'attaque, tanned Marocains and chunky, bull-necked Zouaves, crossed the bridge over the Ornain and marched away. At the turn in the road a new transparency had been erected, with VERDUN printed on it in huge letters. Now and then a soldier, catching sight of it, would nudge his comrade.

On the 18th [of February] we were told to be in readiness to go at any minute and permissions to leave the barrack yard were recalled.

The attack began with an air raid on Bar-le-Duc. I was working on my engine in the sunlit barrack yard when I heard a muffled Pom! somewhere to the right. Two French drivers who were putting a tire on their car jumped up with a "Qu'est-ce que c'est que ça [What is that]?" We stood together looking round. Beyond a wall on the other side of the river great volumes of brownish smoke were rolling up, and high in the air, brown and silvery, like great locusts, were two German aeroplanes.

"Nom d'un chien, il y'en a plusieurs" [Name of a dog, there are more of them!], said one of the Frenchmen, pointing out four, five, seven, nine aeroplanes. One seemed to hang immobile over the barrack yard. I fancy we all had visions of what would hap-

pen if a bomb hit the near-by gasoline reserve. Men ran across
the yard to the shelter of the dormitories; some, caught as we
were in the open, preferred to take a chance on dropping flat under a car. A whistling scream, a kind of shrill, increasing shriek,
sounded in the air and ended in a crash. Smoke rolled up heavily in another direction. Another whistle, another crash, another
and another and another. The last building struck shot up great
tongues of flame.

"C'est la gare [train station]," said somebody. Across the yard
a comrade's arm beckoned me. "Come on, we've got to help put
out the fires!"

The streets were quite deserted; horses and wagons abandoned to their fate were, however, quietly holding their places.
Faces, emotionally divided between fear and strong interest,
peered at us as we ran by, disappearing at the first whistle of
a bomb, for all the world like hermit-crabs into their shells. A
whistle sent us both scurrying into a passageway; the shell fell
with a wicked hiss, and, scattering the paving-stones to the four
winds, blew a shallow crater in the roadway. A big cart horse,
hit in the neck and forelegs by fragments of the shell, screamed
hideously. Right at the bridge, the sentry, an old territorial, was
watching the whole scene from his flimsy box with every appearance of unconcern.

Not the station itself, but a kind of baggage-shed was on fire.
A hose fed by an old-fashioned seesaw pump was being played
on the flames. Officials of the railroad company ran to and fro
shouting unintelligible orders. For five minutes more the German aeroplanes hovered overhead, then slowly melted away
into the sky to the southeast. The raid had lasted, I imagine, just
about twenty minutes.

That night, fearing another raid, all lights were extinguished
in the town and at the barracks. Before rolling up in my blankets,
I went out into the yard to get a few breaths of fresh air. Through
the night air, rising and falling with the wind, I heard in one
of the random silences of the night a low, distant drumming of
artillery (98–100). . . .

The next day at noon, we were ordered to go to Monthai-
ron, and at 12.15 we were in convoy formation in the road by

the barracks wall. The great route nationale from Bar-le-Duc to Verdun runs through a rolling, buff-brown moorland. . . .

Great swathes of barbed wire, a quarter of a mile in width, advancing and retreating, rising and falling with the geographical nature of the defensive position, disappear on both sides to the horizon. And so thick is this wire spread, that after a certain distance the eye fails to distinguish the individual threads and sees only rows of stout black posts filled with a steely, purple mist.

We went through several villages. . . . We dodged interminable motor-convoys carrying troops, the poilus sitting unconcernedly along the benches at the side, their rifles tight between their knees. At midnight we arrived at B——, four miles and a half west of Verdun. The night was clear and bitter cold; the ice-blue winter stars were westering. Refugees tramped past in the darkness. By the sputtering light of a match, I saw a woman go by with a cat in a canary cage; the animal moved uneasily, its eyes shone with fear. A middle-aged soldier went by accompanying an old woman and a young girl. Many pushed baby carriages ahead of them full of knick-knacks and packages (101).

The Battle of Verdun began on February 21, 1916, and lasted until December 18 of that year. In the end, the total casualties at Verdun, killed and wounded for both sides, would come to more than 700,000. For Henry Sheahan and the other ambulance drivers there was endless work, day and night.[7]

From a high hill between B—and Verdun I got my first good look at the bombardment. From the edge of earth and sky, far across the moorlands, ray after ray of violet-white fire made a swift stab at the stars. Mingled with the rays, now seen here, now there, the reddish-violet semicircle of the great mortars flared for the briefest instant above the horizon. From the direction of this inferno came a loud roaring, a rumbling and roaring, increasing in volume—the sound of a great river tossing huge rocks through subterranean abysses. Every little while a great shell, falling in the city, would blow a great hole of white in the night, and so thundering was the crash of arrival that we almost expected to see the city sink into the earth.

Terrible in the desolation of the night, on fire, haunted by specters of wounded men who crept along the narrow lanes by the city walls, Verdun was once more undergoing the destinies of war. The shells were falling along rue Mazel and on the citadel. A group of old houses by the Meuse had burnt to rafters of flickering flame, and as I passed them, one collapsed into the flooded river in a cloud of hissing steam.

In order to escape shells, the wounded were taking the obscure by-ways of the town. Our wounded had started to walk to the ambulance station with the others, but, being weak and exhausted, had collapsed on the way. They were waiting for us at a little house just beyond the walls.

Said one to the other, "As-tu-vu Maurice [Have you seen Maurice]?" and the other answered without any emotion, "Il est mort [He is dead]" (101–102).

The stream of wounded from Verdun seemed endless. The total number of French wounded was, according to the official French war history, 174,973. The French dead or missing numbered 162,308.[8] The château/hospital was a few miles below Verdun on a narrow meadow between the Meuse River and the northern bluffs. Sheahan and the other ambulance drivers came to know it all too well.

The château itself was a huge, three-story box of gray-white stone with a slate roof, a little turret en poivrière [pepper-pot turret] at each corner, and a graceless classic doorway in the principal facade. A wide double gate, with a coronet in a tarnished gold medallion set in the iron arch-piece, gave entrance to the place through a kind of courtyard formed by the rear of the château and the walls of two low wings devoted to the stables and servants' quarters. Within, a high clump of dark-green myrtle, ringed with muddy, rut-scarred turf, marked the theoretical limits of a driveway. Along the right-hand wall stood the rifles of the wounded, and in a corner, a great snarled pile of bayonets, belts, cartridge-boxes, gas-mask satchels, greasy tin boxes of anti-lice ointment, and dented helmets. . . .

A heavy smell of ether and iodoform lay about it, mixed with the smell of the war. This effluvia of an army, mixed with the

sharper reek of anaesthetics, was the atmosphere of the hospital. The great rush of wounded had begun. Every few minutes
the ambulances slopped down a miry byway, and turned in the
gates; tired, putty-faced hospital attendants took out the stretchers and the nouveaux clients; mussy bundles of blue rags and
bloody blankets turned into human beings (104).

The crossroad where the ambulances turned off was a maze
of beams of light from the autos. There was shouting of orders
which nobody could carry out. Wounded, able to walk, passed
through the beams of the lamps, the red of their bloodstains, de-
tached against the white of the bandages, presenting the sharp-
est of contrasts in the silvery glare. At the station, men who had
died in the ambulances were dumped hurriedly in a plot of grass
by the side of the roadway and covered with a blanket. Never
was there seen such a bedlam! (101–102). . . .

Ambulance after ambulance came from the lines full of clients; kindly hands pulled out the stretchers and bore them to the
wash-room, which was in the cellar of the dove-côte. . . . Snip,
snap went the scissors of the brancardiers who looked after the
bath—good souls these two—who slit the uniforms from mangled limbs. The wounded lay naked in their stretchers while the
attendant daubed them with a hot soapy sponge and the blood
ran from their wounds through the stretcher to the floor and
seeped into the cracks of the stones. A lean, bearded man closed
his eyes over the agony of his opened entrails and died there.
Somebody casually tossed a blanket over the body.[9]

[In the driveway] an overworked, nervous médecin chef
shouted contradictory orders at the brancardiers, and passed
into real crises of hysterical rage.

"Avancez! [Forward]" he would scream at the bewildered
chauffeurs of the ambulances; and an instant later, "Reculez! Reculez [Back up]!"

The wounded in the stretchers, strewn along the edges of
the driveway, raised patient, tired eyes at his snarling. Another doctor, a little bearded man wearing a white apron and the
red velvet képi of an army physician, questioned each batch of

new arrivals. Deep lines of fatigue had traced themselves under his kindly eyes; his thin face had a dreadful color. Some of the wounded had turned their eyes from the sun; others, too weak to move, lay stonily blinking. Almost expressionless, silent, they resigned themselves to the attendants as if these men were the deaf ministers of some inexorable power.

The surgeon went from stretcher to stretcher looking at the diagnosis cards attached at the poste de secours [first-aid post], stopping occasionally to ask the fatal question, "As-tu craché du sang?" (Have you spit blood?) A thin oldish man with a face full of hollows like that of an old horse, answered "Oui," faintly. Close by, an artilleryman, whose cannon had burst, looked with calm brown eyes out of a cooked and bluish face. Another, with a soldier's tunic thrown capewise over his naked torso, trembled in his thin blanket, and from the edges of a cotton and lint-pad dressing hastily stuffed upon a shoulder wound, an occasional drop of blood slid down his lean chest (105).

The exhausted ambulance drivers slept when they could, but they did not rest well.

We slept in the loft of one of the buildings that formed the left wing of the courtyard of the castle. To enter it, we had to pass through a kind of lumber-room on the ground floor in which the hospital coffins were kept. Above was a great dim loft, rich in a greasy, stably smell, a smell of horses and sweaty leather, the odor of a dirty harness room. At the end of the room, on a kind of raised platform, which ran along the wall over our heads, was the straw in which we lay—a crazy, sagging shelf, covered with oily dust, bundles of clothes, knapsacks, books, candle-ends, and steel helmets. All night long the horses underneath us squealed, pounded, and kicked.

I see in the lilac dawn of a winter morning the yellow light of an officer's lantern, and hear the call, "Up, boys, there's a call to Bar-le-Duc." The bundles in the dirty blankets groan; unshaven, unwashed faces turn tired eyes to the lantern; some, completely worn out, lie in a kind of sleepy stupor, while a wicked screaming whistle passes over our heads, and the shell, bursting on a near-by location, startles the dawn.

The snow begins to fall again. The river has fallen, and the air is sickish with the dank smell of the uncovered meadows. A regiment on the way to the front has encamped just beyond the hospital. The men are trying to build little shelters. A handful of fagots is blazing in the angle of two walls; a handful of grave-faced men stand round it, stamping their feet. In the hospital yard, the stretcher-bearers unload the body of an officer who has died in the ambulance. The dead man's face is very calm and peaceful, though the bandages indicate terrible wounds. The cannon flashes still jab the snowy sky. . . .

The back of the attack is broken, and we are beginning to get a little rest. But during the first week our cars averaged runs of two hundred miles a day, over roads chewed to pieces, and through very difficult traffic. In several of the villages there were unusually formidable shell gauntlets to be run.[10]

Henry Sheahan wrote of passing through one of these "shell gauntlets" when he was ordered to take three men from the chateau to convalesce at a hospital some miles away.

A highway and an unused railroad, both under heavy fire from German guns on the Hauts de Meuse [upper reaches of the Meuse River], passed behind the château and along the foot of the bluffs. There were a hundred shell holes in the marshes between the road and the river, black-lipped craters in the sedgy green; there were ugly punches in the brown earth of the bluffs, and deep scoops in the surface of the road. The telephone wires, cut by shell fragments, fell in stiff, draping lines to the ground. Every once in a while a shell would fall into the river, causing a silvery-gray geyser to hang for an instant above the green eddies of the Meuse. A certain village along this highway was the focal point of the firing. Many of the houses had been blown to pieces, and fragments of red tile, bits of shiny glass, and lumps of masonry were strewn all over the deserted street.

As I hurried along, two shells came over, one sliding into

the river with a Hip! and the other landing in a house about two hundred yards away. A vast cloud of grayish-black smoke befogged the cottage, and a section of splintered timber came buzzing through the air and fell into a puddle. From the house next to the one struck, a black cat came slinking, paused for an indecisive second in the middle of the street, and ran back again. Through the canvas partition of the ambulance, I heard the voices of my convalescents.

"No more marmites [shells]!" I cried to them as I swung down a road out of shell reach. I little knew what was waiting for us beyond the next village. . . .

A regiment of Zouaves going up to the line was resting at the crossroad, and the regimental wagons, drawn up in waiting line, blocked the narrow road completely. The air was heavy with the musty smell of street mud that never dries during winter time, mixed with the odor of the tired horses, who stood, scarcely moving, backed away from their harnesses against the mire-gripped wagons. Suddenly the order to go on again was given; the carters snapped their whips, the horses pulled, the noisy, lumbering, creaky line moved on, and the men fell in behind, in any order. I started my car again and looked for an opening through the mêlée. Beyond the cross, the road narrowed and flanked one of the southeastern forts of the city. A meadow, which sloped gently upward from the road to the abrupt hillside of the fortress, had been used as a place of encampment and had been trodden into a surface of thick cheesy mire. Here and there were the ashes of fires. There were hundreds of such places round the moorland villages between Verdun and Bar-le-Duc. The fort looked squarely down on Verdun, and over its grassy height came the drumming of the battle, and the frequent crash of big shells falling. In a corner lay the anatomical relics of some horses killed by an air-bomb the day before. And even as I noted them, I heard the muffled Pom! Pom! Pom! of anti-aircraft guns. My back was to the river and I could not see what was going on.

"What is it?" I said to a Zouave who was plodding along beside the ambulance.

"Des Boches—crossing the river."

The regiment plodded on as before. Now and then a soldier would stop and look up at the aeroplanes.

"He's coming!" I heard a voice exclaim.

Suddenly, the adjutant whom I had seen before came galloping down the line, shouting, "Arrêtez! Arrêtez! Pas de mouvement [Stop! Stop! Don't move]!"

A current of tension ran down the troop with as much reality as a current of water runs down hill. I wondered whether the Boche had seen us.

"Is he approaching?" I asked.

"Yes."

Ahead of me was a one-horse wagon, and ahead of that a wagon with two horses carrying the medical supplies. The driver of the latter, an oldish, thick-set, wine-faced fellow, got down an instant from his wagon, looked at the Boche, and resumed his seat. A few seconds later, there sounded the terrifying scream of an air-bomb, a roar, and I found myself in a bitter swirl of smoke. The shell had fallen right between the horses of the two-horse wagon, blowing the animals to pieces, splintering the wagon, and killing the driver. Something sailed swiftly over my head, and landed just behind the ambulance. It was a chunk of the skull of one of the horses. The horse attached to the wagon ahead of me went into a frenzy of fear and backed his wagon into my ambulance, smashing the right lamp. In the twinkling of an eye, the soldiers dispersed. Some ran into the fields. Others crouched in the wayside ditch. A cart upset. Another bomb dropped screaming in a field and burst; a cloud of smoke rolled away down the meadow.

When the excitement had subsided, it was found that a soldier had been wounded. The bodies of the horses were rolled over into the ditch, the wreck of the wagon was dragged to the miry field, and the regiment went on. In a very short time I got to the hospital and delivered my convalescents (104–107). . . .

That night we were given orders to be ready to evacuate the château in case the Boches advanced. The drivers slept in the ambulances, rising at intervals through the night to warm their engines. The buzz of the motors sounded through the tall pines of the château park, drowning out the rumbling of the bombard-

ment and the monotonous roaring of the flood. Now and then a
trench light, rising like a spectral star over the lines on the Hauts
de Meuse, would shine reflected in the river. At intervals attendants carried down the swampy paths to the chapel the bodies
of soldiers who had died during the night. The cannon flashing
was terrific. Just before dawn, half a dozen batteries of "seventy-fives" came in a swift trot down the shelled road; the men
leaned over on their steaming horses, the harnesses rattled and
jingled, and the cavalcade swept on, outlined a splendid instant
against the mortar flashes and the streaks of day (108–109).

The 24th [of February] was the most dreadful day. The wind and
snow swept the heights of the desolate moor, seriously interfer-
ing with the running of the automobiles. Here and there, on a
slope, a lorry was stuck in the slush, though the soldier passengers were out of it and doing their best to push it along. The can-
nonade was still so intense that, in intervals between the heavier
snow-flurries, I could see the stabs of fire in the brownish sky.
Wrapped in sheepskins and muffled to the ears in knitted scarves
that might have come from New England, the territorials who
had charge of the road were filling the ruts with crushed rock.
Exhaustion had begun to tell on the horses; many lay dead and
snowy in the frozen fields. A detachment of khaki-clad, red-fez-
zed colonial troops passed by, bent to the storm. The news was
of the most depressing sort. The wounded could give you only
the story of their part of the line, and you heard over and over
again, "Nous avons reculés [We have retreated]." A detachment
of cavalry was at hand; their casques and dark-blue mantles
gave them a crusading air. And through the increasing cold and
darkness of late afternoon, troops, cannons, horsemen, and mo-
tor-trucks vanished toward the edge of the moor where flashed
with increasing brilliance the rays of the artillery (102–103). . . .

In the afternoon a sergeant rode with me. He was somewhere
between twenty-eight and thirty, thick set of body, with black
hair . . . he was married and had two little boys. At Douaumont,
a fragment of shell had torn open his left hand.

"The Boches are not going to get through up there?"

"Not now. As long as we hold the heights, Verdun is safe. . . . But oh, the people killed! Ça s'accroche aux arbres [That clings to the trees."]

The vagueness of the "ça" had a dreadful quality in it that made you see trees and mangled bodies.

"We had to hold the crest of Douaumont under a terrible fire, and clear the craters on the slope when the Germans tried to fortify them. Our 'seventy-fives' dropped shells into the big craters as I would drop stones into a pond. Pauvres gens."

The phrase had an earth-wide sympathy in it, a feeling that the translation "poor folks" does not render. He had taken part in a strange incident. There had been a terrible corps-à-corps [hand-to-hand combat] in one of the craters which had culminated in a victory for the French; but the lieutenant of his company had left a kinsman behind with the dead and wounded. Two nights later, the officer and the sergeant crawled down the dreadful slope to the crater where the combat had taken place, in the hope of finding the wounded man. They could hear faint cries and moans from the crater before they got to it. The light of a pocket flash-lamp showed them a mass of dead and wounded on the floor of the crater—"un tas de mourants et de cadavres [a heap of the dying and the dead]," as he expressed it.

After a short search, they found the man for whom they were looking; he was still alive but unconscious. They were dragging him out when a German, hideously wounded, begged them to kill him.

"Moi, je n'ai plus jambes [I have no legs]," he repeated in French; "pitie, tuez-moi [have pity, kill me]."

He managed to make the lieutenant see that if he went away and left them, they would all die in the agonies of thirst and open wounds. A little flickering life still lingered in a few. . . . A rafale of shells fell on the slope; the violet glares outlined the mouth of the crater.

"Fermes tes yeux [Close your eyes]," said the lieutenant to the German. The Frenchmen scrambled over the edge of the crater with their unconscious burden, and then, from a little distance, threw hand-grenades into the pit till all the moaning died away.

Two weeks later, when the back of the attack had been broken and the organization of the defense had developed into a trusted routine, I went again to Verdun. The snow was falling heavily, covering the piles of débris and sifting into the black skeletons of the burned houses. Untrodden in the narrow streets lay the white snow. Above the Meuse, above the ugly burned areas in the old town on the slope, rose the shell-spattered walls of the citadel and the cathedral towers of the still, tragic town. The drumming of the bombardment had died away. The river was again in flood. In a deserted wine-shop on a side street well protected from shells by a wall of sandbags was a post of territorials. . . .

"Do you want to see something odd, mon vieux?" said one of the pompiers [firemen] to me; and he led me through a labyrinth of cellars to a cold, deserted house. The snow had blown through the shell-splintered window-panes. In the dining-room stood a table, the cloth was laid and the silver spread; but a green feathery fungus had grown in a dish of food and broken straws of dust floated on the wine in the glasses. The territorial took my arm, his eyes showing the pleasure of my responding curiosity, and whispered,

"There were officers quartered here who were called very suddenly. I saw the servant of one of them yesterday; they have all been killed."

Outside there was not a flash from the batteries on the moor. The snow continued to fall, and darkness, coming on the swift wings of the storm, fell like a mantle over the desolation of the city (110–112).

Henry Sheahan drove an ambulance for the French from September 1915 until February 1916. On April 4 he sailed for home.[11] From his first harrowing night in Paris as the wounded came in from the battle of Champagne, to the trenches of the Bois-le-Prêtre, to the outskirts of Verdun, he had seen a war whose horrors defied description. As for the outcome of that war, as he looked back on its progress in 1916, Sheahan was not hopeful.

Outside of important local gains, the great western offensives have been failures. Champagne was a failure, the Calais drive was a failure, Verdun was a failure, and the drive on the Somme has only bent the lines. The Germans may shorten their lines because of a lack of men, but I firmly believe that neither their line nor the Allies' line will ever be broken. What will be the end if the Allies cannot wrest from Germany, Belgium and that part of northern France she is holding for ransom—to obtain good terms at the peace congress? Is Germany slowly, very slowly going under, or are we going to witness complete European exhaustion? Whatever happens, poor, mourning, desolated France will hold to the end (61).

And "the end" on the Western Front was not yet in sight. From February to December 1916 the struggle for Verdun raged; the Battle of the Somme, from July to November that same year, killed and wounded more than 1 million. The Eastern Front, where Russian troops had been fighting German and Austro-Hungarian forces, was about to collapse. War and domestic unrest in Russia forced a revolution and the abdication of Czar Nicholas II in March 1917. One month earlier, Germany declared unrestricted submarine warfare against all neutral and enemy vessels in the North Atlantic. Finally, in April 1917 President Woodrow ("He Kept Us Out of War") Wilson asked Congress for a declaration of war against Germany. Many Americans, including ex-president Theodore Roosevelt, rejoiced. George M. Cohan wrote a hit song called "Over There," 4.5 million young men entered the armed forces, and 2 million would serve in Europe.[12]

Two of them were George Wythe and Mike Hogg.

The Soldiers
1917–1919

A few weeks after the United States entered World War I, the War Department ordered the creation of thirty-two divisional training camps for troops. There were sixteen tent camps for the National Guard and sixteen camps with wooden buildings for the US Army. The need for trained soldiers was urgent, and the nation's military was woefully unprepared. In 1917 the combined US Army and National Guard numbered slightly over 300,000 men, and the army was just beginning to replace its mules and wagons with trucks. President Wilson's initial call was for 1 million troops. The Selective Service Act of May 18, 1917, required all males between the ages of eighteen and thirty to register. In the end, some 2.8 million men were drafted and another 2 million volunteered.[1]

Six weeks after the United States declared war on Germany, George Wythe, age twenty-four, and Mike Hogg, age thirty-two, were among 2,500 Texans at Camp Funston, a newly opened reserve officer training camp near Leon Springs, Texas. If they made it through the rigorous ninety-day program as "90-day wonders," they would be commissioned as lieutenants in the US Army. In 1917, when he left civilian life, George Wythe was working as an assistant city editor for the *Dallas Morning News*. Mike Hogg was helping his older brother, Will, in family business interests in oil and cotton in Houston. By the summer of 1918 Wythe and Hogg would be commanding troops on the Western Front in France, where they would serve through the end of the war. Major George Wythe would write the official history of the US Army's 90th Division, from its creation at Camp Travis, near San Antonio in 1917, through the Battles of St. Mihiel and the Meuse-Argonne in 1918, to the end of its wartime service in the Army of Occupation in 1919. Captain Mike Hogg, also of the 90th Division, would write letters home, from the time he drilled at Camp Funston in May 1917 to his weeks in the Army of Occupation in postwar Germany in 1919.

Lieutenant Mike Hogg became Captain Mike Hogg on August 15, 1917, and by August 25, he was an officer in the just-created 90th Division at Camp Travis. In September he wrote to his sister, Ima, about his new responsibilities. As Captain Hogg, he commanded Company D of the 1st Battalion, 360th Infantry Regiment, 180th Brigade. The 180th was the Texas Brigade, composed of Mike's 360th Infantry with men from South and East Texas, and the 359th Infantry, with men from North and West Texas. There was also an Oklahoma Brigade, the 179th. Its two regiments, the 357th and the 358th Infantry, were filled with recruits from western and eastern Oklahoma, respectively. At full strength the entire 90th Division would have some 30,000 men. They were among the ninety-three combat divisions organized for the war, forty-two of which were sent to France.[2]

Mike Hogg, 1917. Courtesy of
Museum of Fine Arts, Houston.

Captain Mike Hogg

Mike Hogg was not unfamiliar with the military, having worn a uniform and learned to drill as a boy at the Carlisle School in Hillsboro, Texas. In fact, he had rather liked it. In May 1917 he found himself drilling for real at Camp Funston. He wrote the first of many letters to his sister, Ima, in Houston:

Wednesday [May 1917]
Dear Sis:
This camp thus far, is the greatest experience I have ever had. We get up at 5:40 every morning and, from that time on till six p.m., we are on the "hop." Our equipment is the same as the regular army, and our duties are equally as severe. Everyone is very enthusiastic and, of course, this adds to the interest. We have marching, lectures, music, swimming, and many other things of interest.
Only a few minutes before called out.
With love -
Mike.[3]

On June 9 Mike wrote to Ima that "about two-thirds of those that came over at first will be sent home in the next week. I hope I have made good and won't be in the bunch. I think I have." He already knew how to shoot, from a boyhood of hunting with his father and his two brothers. Now he was aiming to hunt a different kind of game. On May 8, 1917, some 3,000 men had begun three months of intensive training at Camp Funston; 1,846 of them had graduated as second lieutenants on August 15. One was Lieutenant Mike Hogg. His older brother, Will, once described him as "not particularly studious" but "fairly aggressive and industrious."[4] After a two-week leave in Houston, Mike Hogg moved on to Camp Travis, near San Antonio.

Lieutenant George Wythe also graduated from Camp Funston and moved to Camp Travis. A serious young man with a journalist's eye for detail and organization, he was soon promoted to captain and attached to the Depot Brigade, helping process the hundreds of recruits arriving almost daily in the summer of 1917. When the troops went overseas, he served in the 90th Division's 179th Brigade and was promoted to major in October 1918. After the war ended, he was asked to write the official history of the 90th Division. In the spring of 1919 Major Wythe set to work, recording in meticulous detail everything from the earliest days at Camp Travis through the end of the war: how the 30,000 soldiers of the 90th Division trained, ate, slept, and fought. When the work was finished, Lieutenant Colonel Schofield Andrews wrote to Wythe, "You are to be most heartily congratulated on the splendid history which you have written."[5]

Here Wythe describes Camp Travis, a vast expanse of Texas prairie covering 18,290 acres.[6]

[GW] Adjoining the buildings of Fort Sam Houston, on the north-eastern outskirts of the city of San Antonio, the camp embraced all of old Camp Wilson, a National Guard concentration point, and in addition a huge tract of sandy land where nothing save a waste of mesquite brush had existed prior to the erection of the city of wooden barracks. The camp took its name from Lieutenant Colonel W. B. Travis, defender of the Alamo, and was one of the sixteen National Army cantonments erected simultaneously in different parts of the United States.[7]

The 90th Division had its official history, but so did smaller units within that Division: Mike Hogg was in Company D, 360th Infantry. The unnamed author of that unit's history chronicled in minute detail

George Wythe, US passport photo, 1920.

every kilometer, every battle, every casualty of Company D from its formation in the summer of 1917 through the end of the war in November 1918.

[Co. D] Company D was organized at Camp Travis, Texas, August 29th 1917. Captain Mike Hogg was assigned as Company Commander, and Lieutenants Gustave C. Dittmar, Jesse F. Gray, Nelson A. Miller, and Charles H. James were also assigned. By the 15th of October the Company was at full strength, and the task of preparation for service overseas was well underway. [8]

Mike Hogg had four or five lieutenants under his command, and his total company ranged from about 200 to 250. In combat at the Western Front, they were reduced to 115. He led them through some of the fiercest fighting of the war, making light of deprivation and danger, always cheerful. To judge from his letters home, Captain Mike Hogg was both an officer and a gentleman, good-tempered and considerate. His father had written of him at age three, "Without doubt he is a natural born gentleman, without a single dirty spot in his nature. Every one loves him immediately on seeing him."[9] Captain Hogg wrote as often as he could to his sister, Ima.

Sunday, October 7, 1917
Dear Sis:
Here I am, at last, writing you a young letter. I started one several times, but quit before time.
It is needless to say that I have been busy. Besides having to train my Company, I have been getting training. We are having French classes and military classes, one or the other, every night. All of the work there is not nearly so hard as Funston was. Things are going much easier.
My Company had the first formal guard mount at Camp Travis yesterday. It just happened to be my day for guard and I was lucky that it was ordered to be formal. My Company behaved beautifully.
The men of my Company come from East Texas—Trinity County, Angelina, Walker, Montgomery, and Polk. I have only one man who is not a full-blooded American. That is very lucky. Most of the other Companies have Germans, Swedes, Mexicans, etc.
The Camp is moving along in a wonderfully smooth manner. The

Reserve Officers are doing things as if they had been in harness for years. Our Brigade took a nine-mile hike the other day and only twenty-one men out of the six or seven thousand dropped out. I never lost a man. . . . The class of men that we are getting is better than that of the regular army, however, they are not very literate. For instance, there are ten men in my Company who cannot read nor write, and the average grade is about the fifth.[10] All of my men, except about eight, are farmers. You never saw a more willing bunch anywhere. Their spirit is great. You should have seen them when they came to me. They looked like scarecrows. Their hair was long and unkempt. As fast as they came, I had them shaved and their hair cut. They would not even know themselves. You could not believe that they ever looked like they have. They are a fine looking bunch. Lots of six-footers. My barracks is as clean as your music room. Scrub, scrub, scrub, all day long. That's what it takes.

I believe we will be here for five or six months yet. Will try to write every week from now on.

With much love -
Mike.

[Co. D] The adjustment from civil to army life was a grinding ordeal to say the least, yet the spirit and cooperation of the men was such that it was evident Company D would prove of sterling worth when the time to meet the enemy arrived. On December 12th the Company marched to the Division Target Range where it received its first instruction in rifle firing. In addition to target practice, problems and maneuvres were carried out each day, and proved interesting as well as instructive. Classes of instruction in the use of the Browning, Lewis, Chauchat automatic rifles were also held. The Christmas Holidays were spent at the range, and the bitter experience of being away from the home fireside on festive days was an added test to the quality of the men. However, the new interest held sway. About three weeks were spent at Camp Bullis, then the Company moved back to its quarters at Travis.[11]

[GW] There were both comedy and pathos in the episodes which lightened the drudgery of the hard-working receiving officers. The recruits had followed very literally the instructions not to wear to camp any unnecessary clothing. The weather was warm, and some complete uniforms consisted of nothing more than a pair of heavy boots on sockless feet and the all-embracing blue overalls. The amount of baggage varied from a tooth-brush to a steamer trunk.

Those first weeks were strenuous ones. The problem of making a well drilled army out of this formless mass of backward "rookies" was staggering, but the officers were devoted to their task, and the majority of the men were apt and willing. The life of the company officer was a continual round of drills by day and officers' schools at night (7).

There was little time for letter writing in those hectic days at Camp Travis, and most of Captain Hogg's time was spent drilling and studying. An episode of poison ivy and a case of the mumps were news items, but not much else.[12] He was evidently too busy training to comment in his letters on the Bolshevik Revolution in Russia in November 1917, and Germany's truce with the newly formed Union of Soviet Socialist Republics in December of that year. In the spring of 1918 Germany, freed from battles on the Eastern Front, began a new offensive against the Allied forces, mostly British and French, on the Western Front. In the trenches, both sides had suffered devastating losses and were nearing exhaustion. The Americans would not get there in force until July 1918.

Easter Sunday [March 31, 1918]
Dear Sis:
This certainly is a beautiful Easter Sunday.
I finished the Company Commander's school Wednesday. It was a most strenuous and interesting course. We learned a great deal about the modern methods that the French and English are using. Another Captain and myself tied for high place on the examination. Pretty good for an old man, eh?
Well, they have torn things to pieces around here. Most all of our beautifully trained men have been sent away [to fill up Regular

Army and National Guard units]. *Our regiment is shot* [gone] *to pieces. The officers are all here and it is understood that we will be filled up again, meaning that it will be some time before we get across* [to France].

We had an inspection of the Companies of the Division by General Allen [General Henry T. Allen, commander of the 90th Division] *and this Company got a very good report from him.*

I can't imagine what has become of the sweaters you have shipped. I have heard nothing from this end.[13]

The fight "over there" is too big a problem for me to even contemplate, however, I will say that it looks at present as though the Allies have received at least a great set-back. You can never tell, of course. The Germans may have bitten off "too large a hunk."

Though Mike did not know it when he wrote this letter, the massive German offensive on the Western Front would be defeated. American troops would soon make their presence felt in a war where both sides had grown weary of the stalemate in the trenches. But first the untrained Americans had to learn how to fight, to be proficient with rifle, pistol, machine gun, and heavy artillery. And there was trench warfare. At Camp Travis they practiced in trenches dug at nearby Salado Creek. Besides training infantrymen, Camp Travis had to train stable sergeants, saddlers, cobblers, and horseshoers (this army still had need of horses) plus "bakers, teamsters, bandsmen and buglers, mess sergeants, cooks, and company clerks," as George Wythe said.

Captain Hogg was eager for overseas action. Later in April he wrote to his brother, Will, of "hearing rumors of about when we will go." Meanwhile, to pass the time, he and his men, who prided themselves on "having the best singing regiment in Camp," were hearing local talent: "These darn fool civilians, who have singing societies, or think they can sing, are always inviting themselves out to sing. . . . If they just knew how much misery they caused the poor men, not to speak of the officers! We have had the <u>pleasure</u> of hearing everything in San Antonio croak that even has a semblance of a voice. They come to us as flies go to sugar."[14]

Besides singing, there were other diversions at Camp Travis while the soldiers waited to go overseas:

All forms of athletics and sports were encouraged; field days were held; baseball, football, wrestling, basket-ball, tug-of-war, track and military sports found the men's interest on half-holidays and after drill. Here in the open, church services were held every Sunday morning, when the weather permitted, by the 360th Infantry, the entire regiment attending. . . .

In this formative period much stress was laid upon personal appearance and neat uniforms, and there was inaugurated the impressive salute which became famous abroad as the "90th Division salute." The strictest hygienic regulations and a meticulous policing of barracks and grounds were enforced. Grounds surrounding the barracks were ornamented with flowers and shrubbery. . . .

With the completion of the combat problems and maneuvers which followed target practice, the Division was prepared for overseas duty, and every one looked forward to immediate service in France. But then came the first big disappointment. The Division was called upon to give up many of its best men to fill up regular and National Guard divisions, and to form special organizations of S. O. S. [Services of Supply], army, and corps troops. The largest number of transfers was made about March 25 (8). . . .

During the period of a week following June 5 practically every unit left Camp Travis.

All the Division passed through Camp Mills, Long Island, prior to the actual boarding of the transports (13).

[Co. D] Company [D] left Camp Travis June 6th, 1918, enroute to Hoboken, N. Y., and on arriving there it was ordered to Camp Mills,
Long Island, for equipment and inspection.[15]

An undated note to Ima from Mike Hogg on Long Island, waiting to board a ship, reads: "Just got here last night and leaving tonight. . . . No sleep at all last night. Worked all night. . . . Passed right through New York. . . . Will write you every week over there." He sailed for France on June 14, 1918, and wrote to his sister from aboard ship the next day.[16]

Saturday [June 15, 1918]
Dear Sis:

I thought that when we got on here, there would be some let-up in our work, but not so. That seems to be the beginning and ending of everything. However, it is all right. No one is being hurt by it.

Our trip, so far, has been ideal. Practically no one has been sick at all and the water has been as calm as I have ever seen it. I have seen no one who is a bit uneasy about U-Boats. I have questioned my men and not a one has admitted that he had the slightest uneasiness. I believe that if one put a torpedo into us, we would not be a bit alarmed, even then.

We made an almost superhuman "get-away." Ours was the record, so far.

I wish there were more I could tell you, but it can't be done. We are all well and the spirit throughout is wonderful.

With much love -
Mike.

[GW] The Division left America during the period June 13–July 6. Some organizations were lucky enough to make the voyage on big liners such as the *Olympic*, but others had to content themselves with the smaller craft which had been pressed into the transport service on account of the shortage of tonnage. The crossing of the Atlantic was made without the loss of a single life on account of hostile submarine activity, but the passengers of more than one convoy went through the exciting experience of a frustrated submarine attack. Although some units landed directly in France, the majority passed through England, docking at Liverpool or Southampton. From the latter port cross-channel boats were taken for Cherbourg or Le Havre (13).

German submarines, or U-boats, were a constant threat in the North Atlantic. American troops on transatlantic voyages were always in harm's way. Mike's ship docked safely at Southampton, England, on Friday, June 21, and two days later, Captain Hogg was in France.

Somewhere or Anywhere in France
Sunday, June 22nd [June 23, 1918]
Well, sis, here we are on record time. Never felt better. I have not yet got on to exactly the censorship game, so can't say much of anything. Really, though, one does not realize that we are not at home. You see, there are so many of us who are together that know each other. The weather is most beautiful—sunshine, crisp atmosphere, flowers, etc.

The trip had its thrills, but very few.

"Dog-gone it" I wish I could say a few things. One thing, I have entirely too much stuff. I bought a leather vest, like you spoke of, in England and then lost it. I also have a wonderful trench coat.

You should see where I am doing this writing. Am sitting on my what-not on the ground and am using the calf of my leg as a desk. Quite a device, eh?

The French children are the most attractive things (except for the wonderful strawberries). I never noticed before that they (the children) were so attractive and pretty. They are all dressed most becomingly, even the young beggars. How thick they are. I can hear hundreds of them, talking to the officers. They flock to the soldiers from all alleys, etc. They beg to carry your coat, and teach you French, all at the same time.

I don't know when you will get this.
Love -
Mike.

Many villages in Lorraine were full of war-orphaned children. Their fathers were away in the trenches, or dead, and their mothers were often away working in munitions plants. Grandparents looked after the children.[17]

[GW] After a trip in box-cars of approximately thirty hours' duration, the units of the Division were detrained at Recey-sur-Ource or Latrecey, and marched to their first French billets. The training area in which the Division was located was north of Dijon, in the Côte-d'Or Mountains, on the plateau which divides the valley of the Seine from the valley of the Saone. Although this is a relatively poor part of France, these rolling plateau lands were admirably adapted to training purposes. . . .

Headquarters of the 360th Infantry [Mike Hogg's] were opened at Rouvres-sur-Aube (14).

[Co. D] Company [D] arrived at Arbot, Haute-Marne, July lst, and immediately took up a most intensive training schedule. Eight hours a day (Except Sunday) were spent in the grueling routine of bayonet, bombing, and extended order drill.[18]

Somewhere in France
Monday, July 1, 1918
Dear Sis:
I believe this red stuff is wine that I am writing with. It smells like it. My company just arrived at this place at 2 p.m. today. We made a long, hard hike, the kind you read about, to get here—sixteen miles from the station where we detrained. All men carried heavy packs, which, as you know, weigh about seventy pounds. Ours weighed more, because we had extra stuff to carry. However, not one man fell out. Our march was fine. I cannot say too much about the beautiful weather that we have had from the time we left the USA. It has been wonderful. The nights here are quite cool and the days are warm and nothing but sunshine.

It is late spring here and everything is green. The whole country is alive with flowers.

I am trying to learn this <u>lingo</u>. Am doing very well at present. Can say few things and understand more.

We are at last in <u>Billet</u>. I say at last, because we have been having a most strenuous time up to now.

This little place is situated on a beautiful river among the hills. The water is as cold as our ice water. It needs no ice. Our only church must be four or five hundred years old. Last Sunday we had services in a Catholic church, where we were then located. It was very old and quite interesting. The ceremony was performed by a priest, and was impressive. Our band played at intervals during the services.

Our billet is most comfortable. You should see my quarters. I have a great big room, facing right out toward the hills. My door is a large French window. Of course, it is covered with lace, as are my windows. I have a small stone stoop, where I can set my chair and enjoy the scenery. The yard is a most beautiful flower garden. Say, you talk about

China—this must be an old dining room. The walls are covered with all kinds of old dishes. The old lady, when showing me the room, was very proud of her plates. Two old ladies live here. There are ten soldiers in the back and I hold down this room. You should see how these old boys hustle to keep clean, and they manage to do it. Just as soon as we "hit" a camp and get settled, here they come, swarming out with their dirty clothes, scrub-brushes and soap; they find the public wash-house, hole, mud-puddle, creek, or river, and work begins. At night, they usually have a freeze-off themselves.

The people are very appreciative, although they never forget the American ways about money. These fool soldiers pay any price for anything, and, naturally, are charged accordingly.

This band of ours is a great institution. When marching through villages, it always plays. You have no idea the impression it makes. Many of the villages have never had a band anywhere near and others have not had one for years. It has afforded us lots of fun and pleasure.

Our work out here is just as hard as we can stand. Many hours per day. All are doing it, though, and there seems to be nothing hurt by it.

Say, I don't know when this will reach you. I am sending it to brother because he can get it quicker than you. Well I will close; it is now nine-thirty p.m. It will soon be so dark I can't see without a light, and I have only a candle.

With much love -
Mike.

· ·

[GW] The 90th Division was the twenty-second division of the American Expeditionary Forces in order of arrival in France. It reached foreign soil during the dark days when the Germans were making their last desperate efforts on the Marne to break through to Paris, and immediately preceding the Foch counter-attack which marked the turning of the tide. There was always a large crowd at the railway stations in the divisional area each evening at the hour set for the arrival of the little trains which operate in that region, in order to get a copy of the American newspapers distributed by the Red Cross and Y. M. C. A. Each day's developments were followed with intense interest by both officers and men, who now felt that they were very near the Western battle-front.

Although the towns in which the men were billeted were lacking in the sanitary conveniences of modern American cities, and the simple peasant people did not possess the Parisian charms found in wealthier parts of the French Republic, the men of the Division—the first to train in this area—were given a whole-hearted welcome which remained long in their memories. Differences in language mattered little when hearts were united in a common cause. It was in these little villages that the vast majority of the men received their first introduction to French manners and speech. Learning to "parlez-vous" was the occasion of many humorous episodes (14–15).

All of a sudden, 20,000 soldiers from Texas and Oklahoma descended on fifty small French villages in northeastern France.[19] No doubt there were many "humorous episodes."

July 8, 1918

Dear Sis:

We have been having a little rain for the last day or two. I am glad of it. It is the first I have seen for some time. You should see me and my French lessons. Everyone tries to teach it to you and at the same time learn "American"—no, not English—American! I have a beautiful pronunciation, but, alas, no memory. The durn stuff goes in one ear and out the other. At any rate, I can get along. The time I have is, of course, very limited. Only about an hour a day—sometimes not so much. Here is about the way it happens. I leave supper and stroll up a dingy, narrow street for about a half block, turn in a gate of an old rock wall, and there is a French lesson—about two or three officers sitting around an old lady and her daughter. They have French-English books, dictionaries, etc., dating back to the origin of the two languages. They try to go at it scientifically and we break up the party. No books or grammars for us— conversation. Well, I splash and splatter there for a few minutes, then I move on down the street about a block farther. Right in front of the street is another rock wall, with a gate in it. Here, I enter. Another performance and scene much like the first. This all done, I stroll on home—two old ladies all cocked and primed for a small lesson—dictionaries, sentences written in English meet me on my stoop and here we go for a short round or two. Maybe, some day, I will learn something, but I have my doubts.

This old church, which occupies one corner of my yard, was built in 1108—very near as old as our old ruins. There is one about a mile from here built in 900.

We had a very interesting <u>Fourth</u> here. We took our companies over to the next town, where there is a wonderful chateau, and had a regular American field day on the lawn in front of the chateau. By the way, Col. P. [Colonel Howard C. Price, commander of the 360th Regiment, 180th Brigade, 90th Division] *lives with the Duke at the chateau. The Duke and his family are very attractive. He has a son, a lieutenant, home from the front. Then, there is his wife and daughter. The daughter looks a great deal like Laura Burleson* [a Houston friend of Mike's and Ima's]. *The Duke is a very large, handsome man. Nothing like what you would imagine a typical Frenchman to be—very quiet, speaks English perfectly, and acts just as a well-bred American would.*

The Chateau was built in the old Feudal days. There are moats all around, etc. I think the most beautiful part of the whole place are the roads leading to it. Great, large trees, which meet overhead, and make a regular dome about one hundred feet above, are all the way up the lanes till you come, suddenly, to the lawn. Flower beds are at the base of the trees. The interior of the Chateau could not be much more attractive. The fixtures, etc. are an accumulation dating from the Fifteenth Century.

We have received no mail so far. I have an idea that you are up in New Hampshire again this summer. No reason to have such an idea, but you liked it so much before that I thought you would "head" that way. . . .

As for news of any description, we hear none, whatever. You know how ignorant I am, ordinarily, about news. Well, that is no circumstance. Have not seen a newspaper for two weeks, and then it was old. The only thing I know is what has to do with me or my outfit.

Well, goodbye. I hope you and the other members of the family are as well as I am.

With much love -
Mike.

A few days later Mike wrote to his older brother, Will:

Somewhere in France
Sunday, July 14, 1918
Dear Brother:

Today is France's Independence Day. It is at this minute only six-thirty a.m.—however, not so early for our billet. We have done many things before this. We are now shaved up, "polished" up, cleaned up, eaten up, dressed up, keyed up, exercised up, and are ready to enjoy and observe this holiday. At seven-thirty this morning, my Company has an inter-platoon baseball game; much rivalry and much interest will be had.

We all got our mail yesterday, and it was like having a Christmas tree. The men were as happy as children who were getting their first gifts and seeing their first tree. Most everyone got mail. I got your letter and two from Sister. One of hers was written to Camp and the other over here. I suppose Sister told you of the work I was doing before departure. It came out very successfully. In fact, my Company was the best of any, so far as I could figure. Everything is of a different nature here, but no less a "piece of work." My work is most interesting and I am better satisfied with what I am at than I have ever been with anything. The harder it becomes, the more I hope this feeling will grow, because that is the way it should be. Do not misunderstand me. My greatest desire is that this war end as speedily as possible. One is so "hand-tied" by these censorship rules that it is almost impossible to get "anywhere" with what you would like to say. It is really quite exasperating. I could write almost a book of what I would like to say, all of which cannot pass my own censorship. We have made a clean village out of a very filthy one. This is always the rule wherever our troops may be.

By the way, tell Sis not to worry about sending me clothes. It will be some time before it is cold and I already have more than I can, or am allowed to, carry with me.

No chance to have a photo taken. These people never saw a "movie" till the other day. They were very much excited. We have a town crier who announces all the news. He is a queer looking animal. Whenever he has any news or makes an announcement, he dresses up in his best clothes, a derby, wooden shoes, and an old, slick, tight, once-black, but now green, suit. He has a snare drum, which he beats most furiously up and down the street before he makes his news known. Everyone runs out to hear what he has to say. Yesterday, he seemed in a great heat. He was beating his drum, pointing to his left arm, and having a lot to say. I heard at first that one of the soldiers from this town had won the War Cross, then I heard that the French had won a large fight. The truth was that all the children of the town were to be vaccinated that day. So, you see what we do for news, when there is one source for it. No photos near here, however, we are going to get a Kodak and take some small pictures. I think they will be interesting—no backgrounds—just photos of one or two at a time. I have reached the time for the ball game. I have to umpire, so must say goodbye.

With love -

Mike.

Captain Hogg and his men were doing a great deal more than playing softball in France. They were in combat training, not far from the battle lines. But in their off hours they kept their spirits up. On August 11 Mike wrote to Ima that she should "hear these boys down in their billets playing and singing. They are having a glorious time. They have managed to rake up some violins and between songs and yells, they are having some real old-time East Texas break-down music—very typical and surprisingly good."

[GW] During the five weeks the Division remained in this area, it underwent an intensive course of training prescribed by the G. H. Q. [military acronym for "general headquarters"] program. It must be remembered that many of the men were absolutely new recruits, lacking even the rudiments of close order drill, and that during the short time allotted it was necessary to start at the very beginning and carry them through to a condition of preparedness for battle service. Eight hours a day were devoted to drill, bayonet exercises, intrenching, target practice, minor tactics and maneuvers (15). . . .

At last, on August 15, Field Order No. 1, 90th Division, was issued to move to a "new area." Where this area was remained the secret of the staff, the order merely designating the entraining points: Latrecey for the 180th Brigade [Mike Hogg's brigade]; Poinçon-les-Lorrey for the 179th Brigade [George Wythe's brigade] and Châtillon for Division Headquarters, the 315th Engineers, and divisional units. Not until the troops passed through the "regulating station" at Pagny-sur-Meuse, near the end of their journey, were they told their destination.

French troop trains are all alike. They are composed of seventeen box-cars (the famous "8 chevaux ou 40 hommes" [8 horses or 40 men]), thirty flat cars, one worn-out passenger coach for officers, and two service cars. This train is adapted to carry a battalion of infantry, with its baggage and trains, which is the unit of transport. In accordance with French orders, there was a section of machine guns on each train for anti-aircraft defense in case of aerial attack, but the trip passed off without incident. The troops were detrained at Toul, Foug, and Domgermain (17–18).

Under General John J. Pershing, commander of the American Expeditionary Forces (AEF), the American First Army was preparing for the Battle of St. Mihiel. The operation involved 500,000 troops, including 70,000 French. St. Mihiel was a town on the Meuse River, south of the Argonne Forest. It was the key to a vital railroad controlled by the Germans and must be taken by Allies before a main assault on German lines could begin. Besides being the first major conflict involving American troops, St. Mihiel was an airplane battle, with more than 1,400 planes commanded by General William Mitchell. There were also two tank battalions commanded by Colonel George S. Patton.[20]

Captain Mike Hogg was about to enter the notorious Bois-le-Prêtre, retracing some of Henry Sheahan's steps in 1915–1916.

[Co. D] On August 18th the Company left for the front, arriving at Jezainville August 22nd, where the 360th Infantry Regiment took rear positions in the Forêt-de-Puvenelle. The first Battalion [including Company D] remaining in support of the Second Battalion until August 29th, when it took up positions in the front line trenches. The Company remained in the front line for ten days. It was then relieved and returned to its former position in the Forêt-de-Puvenelle. Here it remained two days and then returned to a new position in the front lines. On the morning of September 12th, 5:08 a.m., after a terrific barrage of four hours duration, the Company went "Over the Top" in support of Company B, 360th Infantry. Here the Company suffered its first casualties. Its objective reached by 6:00 a.m., the Brigade had succeeded in ridding the notorious Bois-le-Prêtre of the enemy, and now held the intricate system of trenches and dug-outs that the enemy had held for four years. In attempting to regain this ground, the French in 1915 suffered over one-hundred twenty thousand casualties.[21]

George Wythe described the larger perspective.

[GW] The sector where the Texas and Oklahoma men first entered the battle-front was almost due north of Toul. The right boundary of the Division was about two kilometers [1.2 miles] west of the Moselle River, the front line beginning at a point in the Bois-le-Prêtre about three kilometers [1.9 miles] northwest of Pont-à-Mousson, and extending more than nine kilometers [about 5.5 miles] westward to a point just south of Remenauville. There were German outposts in the ruins of the last-named village (21).

The two regiments of the 180th Brigade took over the trenches running through Bois-Ie-Prêtre, the scene of desperate fighting between the French and Germans in 1915. The action which occurred there was typical of the bitter trench fighting which characterized the year 1915 in the history of the World War. The trenches of the opposing forces were so close together that an ordinary tone of voice in the German trenches would be audible to the French. The struggle never ceased, and the harassing by artillery, hand grenades, machine guns, and raiding parties continued day and night. A gain of a few yards was sometimes warranted of sufficient importance to receive notice in the official communique. During this period what had once been a dense forest was reduced to nothing more than a waste of stumps.

As the sector quieted down, the Germans and French drew further apart. At the time [August 1918] the 90th Division entered the sector, No Man's Land was of an average width of one kilometer [about half a mile], and was filled with the maze of trenches and wire which was once a part of the front line systems (22–23).

On the night of August 21 the Texans had gone into action, under fire for the first time. For the next four weeks they were on patrols day and night.

[GW] The 3d Battalion, 357th Infantry, was the first battalion to enter the line. Its relief was reported complete at one o'clock on the morning of August 22. On the two preceding nights the 3d Battalion had stayed at Francheville and Martin-court, respectively. The 2d Battalion, 359th Infantry, entered the front line the same night, the relief being completed only shortly after that of the 3d Battalion, 357th Infantry. Also that night the 2d Battalion, 358th Infantry, and the 1st Battalion [Mike Hogg commanded Company D of this battalion], 360th Infantry, went into positions on the main line of resistance (24). . . .

In order to mask the coming attack, the sector was kept a "quiet" one. Until the time that the Division began active preparations, the only activities were the usual artillery fire, the daily airplane patrol, and patrol reconnaissances. But those nights in the front line trenches, with nothing separating the occupants from the Boches but terrifying blackness which occasionally took on living form, will long be remembered after more spectacular moments are forgotten. Since the Division had taken over a front of more than nine kilometers, the troops in the outpost garrisons were necessarily widely dispersed. There were naturally some cases of "nervousness," which were given vent in rifle or machine gun fusillades, or in calls for an S. O. S. barrage from the supporting artillery, but it is hard to find fault with over-caution. . . .

Each regiment sent a patrol out to its front nightly to locate the enemy out-posts and ascertain the nature of the hostile defenses. This also served the purpose of acquainting the men with No Man's Land, over which they were later to advance (25–26). . . .

The scene which the divisional sector presented during those last days of preparation was one that beggars description. There was not a nook or cranny, in the woods, behind a ridge, under the cover of a quarry, that did not conceal a battery, a tank, an

ammunition dump, a depot of engineering supplies, or, perhaps, a battalion of infantry. The huge Forêt de Puvenelle, which
seemed to cover half of the divisional area, was alive with the
materials of war. A ride down the Tranchée du Milieu and the
Tranchée de Maidières, roadways which bisected the dense forest, might truly be compared to a visit to a museum in which
had been collected and parked for convenience of inspection all
the latest inventions of the military art.

While no tanks participated on the front of this Division,
the woods within the sector were used as a staging area for the
whippets [light, fast tanks] which were to lead the assault for the
5th Division. Heavy artillery units, both American and French,
began arriving at an early date. Gigantic guns of 9.2-inch caliber
waddled in during the night, and by morning were in a neatly camouflaged position at one side of the road, with the crews
sound asleep in the mud beside them. Sometimes, however,
daybreak still found them a long way from their destination—
perhaps it was engine trouble, perhaps the slippery roads—but
at all events there was only one thing to do, and that was to scur-
ry to the nearest cover before the German aviators came over on
their dawn patrol (28). . . .

The men to whom should go much credit for valiant service
during these nerve-racking days are the drivers of the motor
trucks of the 315th Supply Train. Of necessity, all traffic was under cover of night. And such nights! The volume of rain, which
had been falling steadily for weeks, increased as the day ap-
proached. The slippery roads were jammed with artillery, trucks,
horse transport, automobiles, marching troops, tanks, and on the
edges motorcycle messengers bearing important orders picked
their precarious way. Of course, no lights were allowed, and the
drivers had to follow the muddy, jolty, treacherous roadway as
their "sixth sense" directed them. All would go well until a long
string of trucks met, head on, a similar convoy from the other
direction; then, in the attempt to make the passage, a truck with
its heavy load would "stick" or go in the ditch, and all traffic
was suspended until the machine could be ejected. Often this
was out of the question, and the best that could be done was to
push it as far out of the path as possible and abandon it (28–29).

Driving at night without lights was one of the most dangerous—and most frequent—hazards of the Western Front. In a memoir published in 1918, Robert Whitney Imbrie, an American ambulance driver with the American Field Service, wrote:

> To you gentlemen who have shot rapids, great game, and bil-liards, who have crossed the Painted Desert and the "line," who have punched cows in Arizona and heads in Mile End Road, who have killed moose in New Brunswick and time in Monte Carlo, who have tramped and skied and trekked, to you who have tried these and still crave a sensation, let me recommend night driving without lights over unfamiliar shell-pitted roads, cluttered with traffic, within easy range of the enemy, challenged every now and then by a sentry who has a loaded gun and no compunction in using it. Your car, which in daylight never seems very power-ful, has now become a very juggernaut of force. At the slightest increase of gas it fairly jumps off the road. Throttle down as you may, the speed seems terrific. You find yourself with your head thrust over the wheel, your eyes staring ahead with an intensity which makes them ache—staring ahead into nothing. Now and then the blackness seems, if possible, to become more dense, and you throw out your clutch and on your brake and come to a dead stop, climbing out to find your radiator touching an overturned caisson. Or mayhap a timely gun-flash or the flare of a trench light will show that you are headed off the road and straight for a tree. A little farther on, the way leads up a hill—the pulling of the engine is the only thing that tells you this—and then, just as you top the rise, a star-bomb lights the scene with a dense white glare and the *brancardier* by your side rasps out, "Vite, pour l'amour de Dieu, vite! Ils peuvent nous voir [Quick, for the love of God, quick! They can see us]!"—and you drop down the other side of that hill like the fall of a gun-hammer. Then, in a narrow, mud-gutted lane in front of a dugout, you back and fill and final-ly turn; your bloody load is eased in and you creep back the way you have come, save that now every bump and jolt seems to tear your flesh as you think of those poor, stricken chaps in behind. Yes, there is something of tenseness in lightless night driving un-der such conditions. Try it, gentlemen.[22]

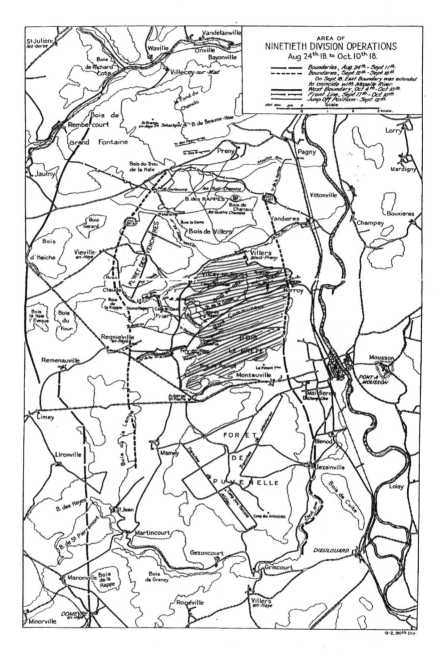

90th Division Operations, August 24–October 10, 1918. Source: Major George Wythe, *History of the 90th Division*, following p. 22.

On September 12, in heavy rain and mud, Mike Hogg's 360th Infantry faced a German network of trenches and barbed wire in part of the Bois-le-Prêtre, in some of the fiercest fighting of the war, and in some of the worst weather: "A wetter, darker, and foggier night could not have been deliberately chosen to begin the offensive."[23]

[GW] During the last few days before the attack, front line battalions were engaged in cleaning out the old French trenches in No Man's Land from which they were to jump off [World War I slang for troops to move forward, beginning an attack] on September 12. During three years of inactivity these trenches had become filled with wire and trash. All the work had to be done silently, under cover of darkness, and the trash had to be disposed of out of sight, as nothing reveals a contemplated attack so readily as the preparation of a jump off line. It was necessary to prepare this departure position very carefully, as the rolling artillery barrage was calculated to fall 500 meters [547 yards] in front of it, and mistakes would mean "shorts" on the heads of our own men. . . .

The assembly of the infantry for the attack was successfully accomplished in spite of difficulties. The night was as black as ink and the rain was coming down in sheets. The positions to be taken up were new to the men, in most cases, and to many of the officers. After floundering about in the mud, stealthily and without light, the men took up their positions before the opening of the artillery bombardment. That artillery preparation was a wonderful thing! It may be doubted if all the firing, terrific as it was, had any material value on our front other than to kill a few Germans. . . . But the sound of the shells whizzing over their heads, and the sight of the flashes of bursting high explosives in Bocheland, cheered the shivering men in the strange trenches, and relieved the strain of the long wait for H-hour (31–32). . . .

Strange as it may seem, the terrific din and awesome splendor of the four-hour cannonading had a soothing effect on the tense nerves of these lads going into their first battle. The German artillery reply had been negligible, as their gunners were too busy at this moment trying to get out of the way. So these Texans and Oklahomans crouched in their trenches, occupied during this fateful period more by curiosity over novel sights than by thoughts of impending action. . . .

The creeping barrage was fired by nine batteries of American 75's and nine batteries of French 75's. The barrage lifted 100 meters [109 yards] at four-minute intervals, a rate which proved a bit too fast for the poor infantrymen who had to cross that sea of wire and trenches and kill a few Boches betimes.

When this barrage had gone forward 500 meters beyond the first day's objective, it stopped and fired so as to form on this line a protective curtain. Behind this rolling barrage bursts of fire from heavier calibers were directed on "sensitive points" such as communication trenches and machine gun positions. At H-hour this "raking fire" dropped on targets near the German front line, lifting as the infantry advanced. Fire for destruction was also carried out on the strong positions in the Bois-le-Prêtre, where stubborn resistance on the second day was feared. . . .

Promptly at five o'clock [a.m.] the irregular belching of the guns was replaced by the rhythmic roll of the 75's, shooting as though in cadence. The barrage had begun—the signal that the supreme moment had come! Simultaneously, the assault troops of the four regiments climbed from the trenches and took up their place in a continuous line that stretched across the divisional front, and formed a part of the 23-kilometer [about 14 miles] wave of men in khaki that engulfed the entire salient [a fortification that juts out to form an angle].

There was no hesitating, no holding back, in all that long line as it moved uniformly across No Man's Land. On the other hand, such was the impetuosity of the supporting troops that they were with difficulty kept at their proper distance to the rear of the front wave, and restrained from joining their comrades on the fighting line.

No one who has ever taken a look at No Man's Land on this front, and seen that twisting, treacherous maze of wire and the hundreds of pitfalls of ancient trenches, has failed to ask how it was possible for human beings to cross such obstacles in the face of hostile fire. French staff officers, sent by Marshal Foch, the Allied Generalissimo, to see this historic region in which thousands of "poilus" had given up their lives to advance the lines a few pitiable inches, gasped in astonishment when they heard of the facility with which American doughboys had surmounted such seemingly unconquerable difficulties. In fact, this achievement will always remain one of the most amazing features of the entire operation; and the modest heroes who accomplished it, on reviewing this land of desolation, themselves wondered just how they did it. But it is sufficient to say that these men from the Southwest were natives of barbed wire's native states!

This problem of the wire was one to which the staff had given considerable thought. For more than a week preceding the attack patrols and working parties had been engaged nightly cutting lanes through the thick bands of entanglements. Owing to the fact that the 5th Division did not take over the front on which it was to attack until nearly midnight, September 11, troops of the 357th Infantry were required to prepare the path for that division as well as for themselves. The men had also been handicapped by a lack of heavy wire-cutters. In their eagerness to supply what was needed, G-1 office almost created a scandal by sending to Nancy, Toul, and neighboring cities to purchase this necessary article of hardware in the open markets. Not until September 10 were efficient cutters received through engineering channels. On the day preceding the attack about 400 of these instruments per brigade were in the hands of the men.

It might be stated that the domestic variety of wire-cutters known to almost every household in the Southwest is only a vest-pocket edition of the "de luxe" reproduction issued on this occasion. The tool was equipped with a handle about eighteen inches long. Little did the Texas and Oklahoma cow-punchers and stock-dealers expect, when they said "good-by" to the Plains to play such a big part on the Western front! (38–40) . . .

In each platoon four men were equipped with the big wire-cutters and told off with the sole mission of cutting wire so that the remainder of the platoon could pass through.[24] This plan worked admirably. The scheme to detail engineers with Bangalore torpedoes to accompany the assault wave for the purpose of blowing up entanglements was carried out, but was not a great success for the reason that from the time that the American and hostile lines drew close together, and the battle waxed hot,

all processes of wire-cutting proved too slow, and each soldier
solved the problem for himself. Here the physical prowess of
the men in the ranks saved the day, and the bands were cleared
at one leap. In the melee the clothes of hundreds were torn to
shreds, and some arrived on the objective so naked that it was
necessary to send them to the rear for a new uniform in order to
avoid freezing. . . .

On the right, the 1st Battalion, 360th Infantry, commanded
by Major W. H. H. Morris, quickly overcame all resistance and
reached its objective by 6:30 a.m. (41).

The lst Battalion, 360th Infantry included Captain Mike Hogg and the
men from Company D. The success of the 90th Division was equaled
by the other divisions farther west, as is evidenced by Field Order No.
51, First Army Corps, issued the afternoon of September 12:

[GW] "1. The enemy has been thoroughly defeated along our
whole front. The number of prisoners taken by the corps amounts
to more than 4000. A number of his guns were also captured. Every objective laid down by the army for two days was attained
in one day under very trying weather conditions. The spirit and
dash shown by the troops is very gratifying to the Corps Commander, and reflects credit upon all concerned." (47). . .

The outstanding feature of the German defense was the organization of the terrain. This [the Bois-le-Prêtre] had been in
1915 one of the most bitterly contested spots on the Western
front, and the elaborate system of artificial defenses which had
resisted the fierce onslaughts of the French, not only were still
intact, but had also been augmented and improved during the
three years of comparative quiet. The trench system extended
seven kilometers [about 4.5 miles] in depth from the front line
to the elements of the Hindenburg line running westward from
the vicinity of Pagny-sur-Moselle. The system consisted of deep
revetted [stone- or cement-lined] trenches and concrete dugouts,
protected by a continuous mass of wire entanglements from one
to two kilometers [0.6 to 1.24 miles] in depth. Even the dewberry
vines conspired to augment the delaying power of these seemingly impregnable lines of defense (47–48).

The Bois-le-Prêtre had been occupied by the Germans since 1915, and by 1918 German troops had settled in, many quite comfortably.

[GW] The dugouts were marvels of comfort and convenience. Slight wonder the Germans had been content to sit down in a period of inactivity for four years and wait. In the Stumpflager, which was taken on the 12th, and at Camp Grollman and in the Norroy Quarries, which fell the second day, were discovered the most perfectly appointed homes, together with large quantities of stores. . . . But the operations were by no means completed by the cutting off of this slice of Bocheland. The same corps field orders which felicitated the troops on the victory contained this second paragraph:

"2. The first phase is now completed. The next step is to organize the line attained for permanent occupancy. This means that the outpost line must be pushed two kilometers in front of the line being fortified and the whole position occupied in depth. This outpost must be established before morning, September 13, and the line of resistance completely laid out and the trenches dug. This position must be held against all attacks of the enemy."

The attack is only half the battle; the modern soldier must know how to wield a spade as well as shoot a gun. There was no chance for rest after the wearying combat of the day. Every one was immediately put to work digging trenches along the line of the first day's objective, which was to be the main line of resistance of the new position. In addition, there was further fighting to be done in establishing the outpost two kilometers beyond the point which had been reached during the first day (47–48). . . .

The greatest advance on September 13 was made by the 360th Infantry, which enveloped practically the entire Bois-le-Prêtre and inscribed the name "Norroy Quarries" on the roll of brilliant achievements of the Texas Brigade (50).

Mike Hogg and his men had acquitted themselves well. George Wythe wrote about the "exploitation" of September 12:

[GW] In drawing the plans for the St. Mihiel operation, the Norroy Quarries had been particularly feared. They were not included in the objectives of the attack, but were left to be dealt with by exploitation. However, on September 12 they were the objects of special consideration on the part of the heavy artillery in order to prepare the way for subsequent operations. Gas troops had also been provided, who promised to drive the garrisons from their defenses. But subsequent investigation showed that the artillery had been unable to make an impression on the German defenses, which included mined dugouts forty feet deep. Furthermore, the gassing program fell through on account of the fact that the first projector touched off blew up, killing the lieutenant in charge and many of his men.

Receiving permission the night of September 12 to exploit, General [Ulysses Grant] McAlexander organized an operation the purpose of which was to seize all the high ground south of Trey valley. The brigade was given the direct support of a battalion of howitzers, in addition to the light regiment covering the brigade front. The 360th Infantry was selected to make the attack (50–51).

The notorious Bois-le-Prêtre had been the scene of some of the bloodiest fighting of the war. In 1915 the French attacked with violence, in hopes of getting through the woods and working down the ravines toward the Moselle. The battle continued for months, and gains were measured in terms of yards. Later the Germans counter-attacked and wrested away all that had been won from them. The French are reported to have lost 123,000 men, of whom 18,000 were killed, in this area. When all advance ceased in 1915, the opposing trenches were so close together that a sound above a whisper could be heard by the enemy. Gradually the contending forces pulled their outposts back, leaving a maze of trenches in No Man's Land (50).

Mike Hogg fought on the ground where Henry Sheahan had been three years earlier, in the area called Quart-en-Réserve, a deadly network of trenches and barbed wire below a commanding ridge in the Bois-le-Prêtre. Henry Sheahan wrote about this place in 1916: "Imagine such a situation complicated by offensive and counter-offensive, during which the French have seized part of the hills and the German part of the plain, till the whole region is a madman's maze of barbed wire, earthy lines, trenches,—some of them untenable by either side and still full of the dead who fell in the last combat,—shell holes, and fortified craters. Such was something of the situation in that wind-swept plain at the edge of the Bois-le-Prêtre."[25] It was the same in 1918. The Quart-en-Réserve was also the location of the rubble that had once been the village of Fey-en-Haye. After the battle, the Americans made use of what the Germans had left behind in the Bois-le-Prêtre.

[GW] Large quantities of stores, especially medical supplies and machine gun parts and ammunition, were captured. Among the spoils were minenwerfer [mortars], gas projectors, grenades, telephone repair kits, signal outfits, and German rations and equipment. The German dugouts, which had been abandoned in haste, provided the victorious Americans the most comfortable quarters they had enjoyed for many a day. There were recreation rooms with pianos and talking-machines intact; handsomely furnished dining-rooms with beautiful serving sets; and offices equipped with every convenience (48, 50–51).

Just as the attack of September 12 was the first experience of the 90th Division in offensive tactics, so it was the initial attempt of the American Expeditionary Forces at large-scale operations. Prior to that date American divisions, and even corps, had played their part at critical moments along different parts of the Allied line. But it was not until the latter part of August that the training of all branches had reached a point that made possible the organization of the First American Army.

An army, it must be understood, is more than a collection of divisions. In the first place, there must be a staff accustomed to handling large-scale operations. General John J. Pershing, commander-in-chief of the A. E. F., himself took command of the army for this first operation [the Battle of St. Mihiel]. There must be railroads and lines of communication, and depots of supplies of all sorts, and experienced officers who know how to get those supplies forward to the fighting organizations. Then there is the aviation service, the tank corps, the long guns of the artillery, the increased medical personnel and hospitals and supplies, engineers to rebuild the roads and railroads as the advance progresses, not to mention the hundreds of military police required for the control of traffic and the evacuation of prisoners, and the salvage squads which reclaimed and saved the debris of battle. In all, there were about 216,000 American and 48,000 French troops in line, and about 190,000 American troops in reserve (32).

Preceding the general advance ordered for the morning of September 15, strong patrols from both regiments aggressively scoured the country to the front during the night of September 14–15. In the 359th Infantry four platoons, one from each company of the 1st Battalion, were employed on this mission. . . . While the 1st Battalion, 360th Infantry was moving forward on the night of September 14–15 to the jumping-off position in the woods overlooking Villers-sous-Preny, patrols from the 2d and 3d Battalions were paving the way for its operations on the following day (55). . . .

As a result of these courageous enterprises, the 1st Battalion was able to advance on the morning of September 15 without the stiff machine gun fire which would have proved deadly on any attempt to cross the open valley. By 10 a.m. the battalion had occupied the outpost position from Côte [Hill] 327 to the point in the Bois des Rappes where contact was made with the 359th Infantry, and had reinforced the platoons of the 3d Battalion on Côte 327 itself. This movement across the valley naturally drew heavy artillery fire, and the outpost positions both in the region of Côte 327 and in the Bois de Chenaux were heavily bombarded. . . .

Upon relieving the 82d Division west of the Moselle on the night of September 16–17, the 360th Infantry established outposts in Vandières (59).

[Co. D] During the reduction of the St. Mihiel salient Company D had five men killed and thirty eight wounded. It lost two officers, Lt. Frank Mulberry, being gassed, September 12, and Lt. Adolph
Fischer, wounded, September 15th.[26]

The Battle of St. Mihiel was over, and the Americans had won.[27]

[GW] It is in the story of battalions advancing in an unbroken wave under a rolling barrage, or the description of the maneuvers of combat groups to outflank deadly machine gun positions, or the narration of heroic exploits of patrols, that everyone expects to find the dramatic and spectacular incidents of war. But any divisional history which relates nothing more than the actual clashes of Americans and Germans must necessarily be incomplete. A division is more than its infantry, artillery, and numerous auxiliary arms. The trains and other organizations which keep the fighting men supplied with food and water, which replenish the ammunition belt when clips are running short, which insure clothing and essential articles of equipment, and which transport the fighting man to the spot where he can fight, are an integral part of the battle machine.

The successive steps in getting food and ammunition forward from the point to which it is brought by railway until it is delivered into the hands of the men in the front line companies form a chain which may be designated as the "system of supply." Nor is the history of the organizations which constitute the links in that chain lacking in situations as tragic, as noteworthy, as humorous as are to be found in the annals of the war.

The point at which the Division's interest in this supply system begins is as far back as the "regulating station," where the daily pack-trains for divisions at the front are made up and routed. These trains, made up of cars of beef, bread, potatoes, hay, and other articles of rations and forage, were despatched daily to a railhead in the area of the division to which they were assigned, and at this railhead were unloaded the supplies to be stored in the railhead dump.

When the 90th Division first went into the line, the regulating station of the 1st Army was near Is-sur-Tille, a little town north of Dijon, where vast warehouses and shops had been erected and which had become one of the most important points on the American Expeditionary Forces' lines of communication, which ran from the base ports through Tours up to the American front in Lorraine (131–132). . . .

The memorable period preceding the attack was one that the drivers of the supply train have particular occasion to remember. The establishment of forward dumps in preparation for the offensive necessitated an unusually heavy traffic over all roads, particularly through the Forêt de Puvenelle, where many of the dumps were located. All hauling was done in the night, without lights, over roads which had been rendered slippery and treacherous by constant rains. In the blackness of the dense woods, with heavy traffic in both directions, many drivers allowed the trucks to get an inch too close to the ditch and were soon capsized. Each morning there were a certain number still stuck in the mud, which the drivers had been unable to extricate before daybreak. The supply train went into the operation handicapped both in trucks and experienced personnel. On September 12 the Division had of its authorized allowance only 65 per cent, of serviceable motor-cars, 55 per cent, of serviceable trucks, and 53 per cent, of serviceable motorcycles (135). . . .

Too much credit cannot be given the wagoners of the regimental supply companies, who kept close on the heels of the fast advancing infantrymen with rolling kitchens, ration carts, and water carts. No division in the American Expeditionary Forces made a better record in getting hot food up to the men immediately after the fight. This was achieved in spite of the condition of the roads. No less important was the hauling forward of munitions. These achievements are noteworthy when it is recalled that both horses and drivers were frequently killed. In no class of men was a stoical disregard for danger and hardship more evident than in the attitude of these drivers, the majority of whom had grown to manhood on the plains and stock farms of Texas and Oklahoma. Wagoner Andrew Pennell, Supply Company, 358th Infantry, illustrates this characteristic unconcern for peril when duty is involved. While driving [his wagon] along a shell-swept road with supplies for the front, he was stopped by an M. P. [military policeman], who said:

"You can't go up that road; it's too dangerous."

"Your road?" inquired Pennell.

"I'm in charge," said the M. P.

"Well, the Germans are shelling the devil out of it back a-ways, and if it's yourn, you had better go look after it."

With this parting shot, the wagoner slapped his wheel team with the reins and was soon out of view on the road, on which shells were dropping intermittently (61–62). . . .

In preparing for the St. Mihiel drive, every precaution was taken to insure the fighting men hot meals as frequently as the tactical situation allowed them to lay aside the rifle and take up the mess kit. The field trains, loaded with two days' field rations and one day's reserve rations, and the rolling kitchens, carrying one day's field rations, were as near the front line as conditions would warrant when the infantry jumped off, and followed up the advancing battalions as soon as roads could be built across No Man's Land. Of course, during the first twenty-four hours after the attack was launched at 5 a.m., September 12, the soldiers ate the lunch they carried, and drew on two days' "iron" rations of hardtack and bacon. In the afternoon of the second day hot food had been got up to the troops of the 357th Infantry, and by that night a roadway had been constructed north from Fey-en-Haye, so that the kitchens of the 358th Infantry were established, on the morning of September 14, at the south edge of Bois de Frière, which had been captured by the 2d Battalion on the previous day. Thanks to better roads in the 180th Brigade sector and the shorter advance on September 12, the problem of supplying the men of the 359th and 360th Infantry was not so difficult at the beginning (136). . . .

Immediately preceding the attack an extra supply of ammunition was delivered to the front line units, so that every man went over the top with 220 rounds S. A. A [small-arms ammunition], and two O. F. [offensive fragmentation] grenades.[28] It was also necessary to supply ammunition for pistols, rifles, grenades, machine guns, Stokes mortars, and one-pounders [thirty-seven-millimeter cannons firing shells with one-pound explosive charges]; flares with which to signal to aeroplanes (138).

While an attack was in progress, the medical teams went into action. A battalion surgeon's diary of the first day of combat during the Battle of St. Mihiel tells the story:

[GW] "The night of September 11, 1918, the medical detachment of my battalion moved forward from its position in support to the front line trenches. The night was very dark, there was a continuous downpour of rain, and we were compelled to advance under a most terrific shell fire. We reached our position about four o'clock on the morning of September 12. As the battalion went over the top in the early morning hours we established our first-aid station in the trench from which they advanced. The first-aid men and stretcher-bearers went over with the first wave, these men being continuously on the field with the infantry. Many times the first-aid men would drag men to shell-holes and administer first aid, being compelled to leave them there until nightfall before being able to litter them to the advance dressing station, on account of sniping, as they were under direct observation of the enemy. This first day we had great trouble in getting our wounded to the rear on account of the endless barbed wire entanglements, and also on account of continuous shell fire all day long, making it impossible for ambulances to push near the station. For this reason the ambulance-bearer section was compelled to litter wounded from my station over the worst possible sort of terrain and under heavy fire a distance of two kilometers [1.2 miles]" (165).

On September 18 Major General Henry T. Allen wrote to his wife about the 90th Division's "baptism of fire" in the September 12 battle:

Nothing could well describe the pandemonium when our artillery began at one in the morning. . . . The night was black and rainy and the bombardment lasted 4 hours when our men *jumped off* behind an artillery fire which continued for 2 hours and 48 minutes. . . . We went into and through and over wires and trenches. . . . I have been through these woods since and the difficulties our men overcame are amazing. This is about one week since the beginning and we are still fighting some to hold our advances. The engagement or rather battle lasted about 3 days. Although our casualties have been heavy they were small for the results obtained. . . . Many of our wounded were light cases. I was told three days since that 500 of them would be out of the hospitals in five days. . . . Many of my men have not yet had their clothes off and of course the shelling continues here and there.[29]

The battle was over, but the work was not done:

[GW] The period of stabilization from September 16 until the relief by the 7th Division on October 10 was one of the most trying in the Division's history. A short time before the relief took place every one was beginning to settle down fairly comfortably, but the organization of the new sector, which took the name of "Puvenelle" from the huge forest, was by no means a simple task. In the first place, the defense of the sector had to be prepared. Colonel F. A. Pope, the Division engineer, immediately sited the main line of resistance, which was to run from the western boundary of the Division along the south bank of the ravine which cut through the middle of the Forêt des Venchères, thence along the north edge of the Bois de Frières to La Poêle, the maze of German trenches which had become famous in the fighting on September 12, here connecting with other German trenches, the Tranchée de la Combe and the Tranchée de Plateau, which were faced in the opposite direction. This work was supervised by the engineers, but most of the manual labor had to be done by the doughboys, who were already exhausted after four days' fighting. . . .

Even more difficulty was experienced in the outpost zone. The men had not yet learned that digging a hole and crawling into it was just as important a part of modern warfare as shooting the enemy. They were perfectly willing to go out on patrols, or make a new advance, if necessary, but trench digging did not appeal to them as the soldierly thing to do. The consequence was very serious, as all the front areas were very heavily shelled, and the men were without adequate protection from shell fire. The Germans were well acquainted with every path and lane through the Bois des Rappes, and were very clever in calculating just the right hour to plaster them with high explosives (63).

German shelling continued from artillery east of the Moselle River. Major General Allen estimated 2,500 shells in one day. There were deadly mustard gas shells as well, causing as many as 1,100 gas casualties in the Division.[30]

[Co. D] September 15th, the advance of the First Battalion was continued, this time the Company [D] being in the assaulting wave. Advancing under a huge enemy barrage, the Company moved forward and by 9:00 a.m. had succeeded in establishing a position on Hill 527, which was the objective. Here it remained until it was relieved by the Second Battalion, and returned to Jezainville for a well-earned rest. After a week's rest the First Battalion relieved the Second Battalion, occupying a support position in the quarries near Norroy. This position being under enemy observation was an excellent target for the enemy, and here he concentrated a harassing barrage each day. At the end of seven days the First Battalion was relieved by the Second Battalion in the front lines. Here the Company occupied the saddle between Hill 527 and Bois-des-Rappes. The Company remained here until October 9th, when the Division was relieved by the 7th Division.[31]

During this brief "period of stabilization" Mike Hogg found time to write to Ima, describing with cheerful insouciance what had been a harrowing combat experience.

Monday, September 23rd
Dear Sis:
You should see me right now. Here I sit, just after having taken the most glorious bath I have ever had. Not that it was up to date, or that I had a good tub, or that I had lots of water. It was a bath—that is all. I am in an old, shell-torn town. The room here is about the only thing left of the house that is whole. The rest has been blown away by shells. This room, however, is great. It can't rain in here. All my officers (four of us) are here.

You are wondering, no doubt, why that bath was so wonderful. Well, it is this way: I am just back from that big American "push"— *St. Mihiel. We were in it up to our eyes. Almost two weeks, we dug, marched, fought and scrambled around in something I know was worse than Hell itself. But here we are, as happy as if we all had good sense— men and all.*

My clean clothes have not yet arrived, but I am sitting here in (marvel of marvels!) clean underwear and clean socks. I rustled them, somehow. My stuff will be here, I hope, today. In the meantime, I refuse to wear what I have. I just shed the dirtiest and most torn up lot of clothes you ever saw.

[GW] Many of the men's uniforms were in rags, and underclothing had become ridden with "cooties [lice]." Beginning immediately after the conclusion of the offensive operations, practically the entire enlisted personnel of the Division was passed through the baths at Griscourt before the Division left the St. Mihiel sector. At the baths every man discarded his old underwear and received a new suit. In addition, new blouses and shoes. Before the attack the men's shelter-half [half of a two-man pup tent], blankets, overcoats, extra underwear, and shoes had been tied in bundles, marked with the soldiers' names, and collected into battalion dumps. When the situation became stabilized, these packs were hauled forward and distributed to the men (139–140).

Mike's letter of September 23, continued:

We have been in the "din" of things now for a month.

Just now, Sgt. Holloman came along with some clippers and gave me a good haircut—in fact, we have all just had that job finished. Still, my clothes have not come and I am as before—clean, with clean underwear. Yes, here is Sgt. Bowman now. He has cake, or cookies and chocolate from the Y.M.C.A. You should see us go after it. Our "Y" man—forty-six years old—a Presbyterian preacher—is one of the greatest fellows you ever saw. If all of the battalions have fared as well as ours at the hands of the Y.M.C.A., words cannot express the great work they are doing. We got a tooth full of candy and cake even while we were fighting. Old Man "Moe" would come stumbling along with chocolate and cake.

Ah! Here are my clothes. I must stop for a few minutes. You know it is rather chilly up here. A series of shivers are playing up my back right now. Gee! I have my clothes on. You never saw me look so "spick and span." I am wearing soft Cordovan shoes and puttees. My uniform is the prettiest I have seen—"Bedford Whipcord." Ye Gods! How fast these things are coming! Here is an order taking Lt. Dittmar from me. He has been marvelous. I believe he is the best officer I have ever seen—a real genius. He now commands Company C. Lt. Burke comes back tomorrow. He has been to school. Lt. Gray and two other Lts. from the Company were wounded. Lt. Jones is still with me and is doing good work.

I have received a great many letters from you. I don't understand why you have not heard more often from me. I have written only once, however, since we came up here. There has been little, or no, chance. The last letter that I wrote was interrupted several times by shells which were falling not too far from my dugout—such as it was.

You asked me many questions in your last letter about canteens, etc. Well, sis, I can see by your questions that you have absolutely no conception of how things are here. We get chocolate, chewing gum, tobacco, cakes, newspapers, etc. Uncle Sam is very good to the boys. They get plenty to eat and plenty to wear. I don't see how any soldiers could be better taken care of.

Imagine Grandpa's place in Wood County, with almost mountains thrown in, and woods about twice as thick, and you have a picture of about how we are situated over here. You can exaggerate your imagination as much as you please and I don't believe you can get too strong of an idea as to it all.

This "over the top" business: Well, about three hours after we had trudged through the darkest night in the most down-pouring rain, and had just got settled in our position, all Hell broke loose. Our artillery had opened up. There we sat, and shivered in water up to our knees. Just as day broke, over we went. I am enclosing a cartoon that most vividly represents what we did until we got our objective.[32] We went through barbed wire, shell holes filled with water, tree tops, logs, blackberry vines, shell fire, machine guns, etc. But Oh My! After we did get to that place—how those dirty cowards "picked" at us with artillery. That seems all they know these days. We did the same thing two days later. Sis, nothing but death itself can stop these marvelous boys. You can tear all but one out of a squad and he will go on as if nothing had happened.

We are here for a few days and back again we go. We are all happy —no one is sick, and there are very few colds. The men are in better health, by far, than they were at Camp.

Of course, this note is not for publication in any sense of the word.

I will write as often as possible. Except for this month, you have received at least one letter a week from me. That is, I have written that many.

My goodness, from the looks of things, all the world is getting married at home. Never mind—we will certainly enjoy life when this thing is over. I really believe I can appreciate a little of it now. Just think—I have been absolutely tied down for nearly a year and a half. Well, sis, show this to brother. He may think I have forgotten him, but he is always included in all my thoughts. He is the sweetest old fellow in the world.

With much love -

Mike.

Mike wrote a newsy letter, but he did not tell his sister everything.

[GW] The divisional front was far from quiet. Every opportunity to harass the Germans was seized. Almost nightly patrols, often in strength, went out from each regimental front with the mission of penetrating as far as possible into the enemy lines, securing information about their defenses, and capturing prisoners. . . . The aggressive spirit of the officers composing these nightly raiding parties is illustrated by the action of Lieutenant (later Captain) James A. Baker, Jr., who never failed to bring back a prisoner (66).[33]

Mike also wrote to his brother, Will, during this period, describing what he had refrained from telling their sister: he was still in harm's way and under fire. Though he was not yet a part of it, the next great battle for the Americans would be the Meuse-Argonne offensive of September 26 to November 11, 1918. To this day, the Meuse-Argonne remains the largest and deadliest battle in American history. It was fought on a battlefront that stretched over 120 kilometers (about 75 miles), involved 1.2 million Americans, killed 26,277, and wounded 95,786. Total American casualties were 117,000; French, 70,000; and German, 100,000.[34]

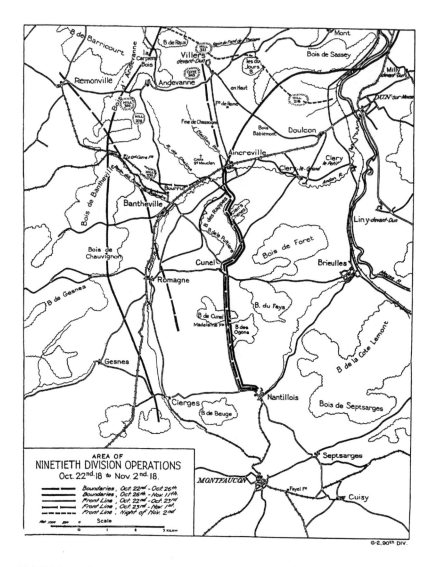

90th Division Operations, October 22–November 2, 1918. Source: Major George Wythe, *History of the 90th Division*, following p. 140.

As troops began moving into place before the Meuse-Argonne battle began, an army surgeon wrote in his diary on September 24, imagining "500,000 armed human beings accompanied by acres of guns. . . a blanket of destruction ten miles deep, thirty miles long, gliding by inches . . . a sheet of death moving at night."[35]

[GW] On September 26 the First United States Army was to attack between the Meuse and the western edge of the Argonne, and the French Fourth Army was to extend operations in eastern Champagne to the Suippe River (78).

On the day the Battle of the Meuse-Argonne began, Mike Hogg, soon to be part of it, wrote to his brother:

Thursday, September 26th
Dear Brother:
Have been having a few days in which to merely draw breath. For sometime now, the sound of things, which are anything but pleasant, constantly greeted my ears. Most of the time, it has been sight as well as sound. I wrote Sister a couple of days ago about going "over the top." That was written the day I got back, so you had better see that. . . .

Say, if you are making any plans for me when I get home, you had better count out an indefinite period, because I am certainly going to take things easy for a while. I am going to lead a real simple life for a while. This year and some months of complete concentration and what is to follow, will seem like an eternity to one, and just a simple little irresponsible rest will be the most glorious thing I can imagine.

We are all in splendid spirits and health. We have lots of fun, even in the most trying times. We boys are well fed and well taken care of. Say, you should hear these old "Whiz Bangs" screech by this window every few minutes. One naturally crawls in his shell—particularly when they fall only a few hundred feet away. You can never tell when one will pay you a quiet visit.

I have not heard a word from Raymond. What Division is he in? If I remember correctly, he is with the Fifth. If that is so, I guess we have been pretty close together recently. I would certainly like to see him. . . .

Well, this experience is worth most everything. I don't just exactly "savvy" the progress of things just now. It seems too good to be true to me. Maybe I am a pessimist. Let us hope so.

Take care of yourself and start that golf game. It will be most glorious for you and your happiness. I am sure it will. I think I am in a position now to tell you that it is worthwhile.

I just stopped here. A damn Boche plane just brought down an observation balloon almost over my head. It fired its machine gun into the balloon and up she went, in flames. The observer jumped out and went sailing over a hill in his parachute. Quite exciting. The whole job did not take five minutes—a common occurrence.

Say, I have a "striker" [officer's servant] that I am going to try to keep always.[36] *He is a little French-American. A perfect wonder. He keeps my things and me too. You should see him go over the top. Well, anyway, when you look for me, look for him, too. He'll be there.*[37]

I will close for this time.

With much love -

Mike.

October 1, 1918

Dear Brother:

Here I sit in this musty old dugout. Under my feet is a burning can of solidified alcohol. Gee! It is great! Over my head is about twenty feet of solid rock. Ah!—the best of all—for not far above that old Fritz is passing them over and dropping over and dropping them in. You know the sound elevated railways make—well, and then some, and you have what has become to me, in these parts, a thoroughly familiar, if not wholly welcome sound. Ah, ha! Say, guess what I have on my head. I have just thought of that. Here I sit with a real "stove-pipe" hat on. We picked it up somewhere in the flim-flam. They all say I look natural in it.

Well, to go back—I have learned to sympathize with wildcats, coons, and all hunted animals. I'll never run them again. You know I have to leave my hole to look things over once in a while and then your wild animal stunt—that is, if it is a pretty clear day. About the time you think all is well, old Fritz has spied you from a "sausage" and here they come, whiz, bang, zip, zam! You run like hell for about a hundred (that is, when you have your first few experiences), then stop, wipe your brow, laugh, cuss the Hun, and then move contentedly on—about that time, sure enough Hell breaks loose all around you. You leap for cover, which might be only a pile of brush, a roll of barbed wire, or anything; you hug the ground and flatten out flatter than anything in the world; Fritz splashes them for a time and then all is quiet again. How the Hell they missed you, you can't tell, because you have merely been playing the ostrich. Now, take it from me, from this time _out_ there is no slow movement. These old-time wildcat movements ensue and remain till back to your beautiful dugout (with its friendly fleas and everything else thrown in) you scramble—and when there, you are as happy as a fool.

We had a good time down here last night. My _runners_ have a fine quartet and how they did sing! We had the latest from Broadway down to our war songs. Some wanted to drop in a few sentimentals but they did not get far.

Old winter is just beginning to show us a few of her less dangerous teeth. The wind is from the north, is rather chilly, and most of the time it mists. It will not be long now before we look for snow. I think we will be thoroughly comfortable. It looks that way to me.

Watch out!—my man, DeLong Champ, is just cutting me some real Dutch cheese. It smells like Limburger. It sure looks good. Oh, we have hot meals and real, genuine, go-getting hot coffee. This cheese stuff is something new. We picked it. No beer, etc. Dam! [sic]. Here is a runner with forty bars of real, live American chocolate—not so bad, eh? You know, this candy follows us, no matter where we go. Personally, I am sick of it, but, I use every effort to keep it supplied to the men. They have their bellies full of it and still crave more. It seems to me that there might be as much effort put into something else and more use gotten out of it.

I have not shaved today and I don't think I shall.

So are you within the draft age now? Sister said something about your going to enlist in the ranks. Well, I think that is far-fetched, because you are of much more service to the Government in other capacities.

It may be that the laws now require an enlistment. It must be, or I am sure that you have better judgment not to say sense, than to enter the ranks. There is no better place in the world than the ranks for those who are fitted for them. No one on earth is better than a good soldier, or, I might say, as good. They have the honor all right, but you are no soldier of the "rank variety," so if the opportunity offers itself, let your patriotic zeal be turned to other lines.

Well, here is chow—wait a minute and I'll tell you what it is. Red beans, condensed milk, tomatoes, coffee, fine bread, coffee—all everything hot—good Lord, here is beef and dumplings, too. Think of it, and here we are biting old Fritz on the heel.

Goodbye, I must eat. With love -
Mike.
P.S. It is sleeting at this minute—ugh!

[GW] The American High Command, fully acquainted with the factors which were rapidly weakening the enemy resistance, had determined not to lose a minute and were pressing the attack in the Meuse-Argonne sector with every available resource. The 90th Division, which had proved its capabilities in the St. Mihiel attack, had been withdrawn, not to rest, but to take station at the "post of honor" on the Meuse. Therefore, before the last units had reached the staging area west of Toul, orders were received to move by "bus" to a region west of Verdun. . . . It was not until October 16 that the 180th Brigade arrived and was billeted in barracks at Jouy, Rampont, and neighboring camps (75–76).

The wet weather in mid-October added to the woes of the troops in their new locations.

[GW] Villages, woods, roads—in fact, every conceivable landmark—had been virtually obliterated. The rain continued steadily and a particularly vicious variety of mud weighted down the feet of the infantry men and clogged the wheels of the regimental trains. Scattering shell fire was incessant, a direct hit dropping on a rolling kitchen and its tell-tale queue of soldiers lined up to receive their allowance of "slum." More times than once in the history of the Division enemy planes spotted this line of flashing mess kit, and sent a wireless flash to a waiting battery, which, by means of the code coordinates of the map thus transmitted by electricity, was able to locate and scatter the dinner party very effectually. . . .

This same day [October 19] the headquarters of the Division moved to Cuisy. The desolation of this region defies description. As for the ancient village of Cuisy itself—well, even Fey-en-Haye was a metropolis in comparison. The only possible simile for the town might be a community of prairie-dog holes out on the Llano Estacado [Spanish for "Staked Plain," known in West Texas as "Great Plain"], for the Cuisy of buildings and streets and homes had ceased to exist, and in its place was a scattered collection of dugouts (80–81). . . .

But there is one point on which the comparison broke down: the Great Plain is dry, but all this area into which the Division was now moving was a lake of mud, churned into slush by shell fire and traffic (82). . . .

Nor was life still further to the rear any more pleasant. The headquarters of the 180th Brigade [Mike Hogg's], in Nantillois, were continually shelled. . . . The Montfaucon-Nantillois-Cunel road was constantly harassed, particularly in the vicinity of the junction of the Nantillois-Cunel and the Nantillois-Cierges roads. There were ammunition and food dumps near this junction. Field Hospital No. 360, which was also in this neighborhood, suffered from the searching artillery fire on October 25. . . .

The operations were only a prelude to the general attack on the army front on November 1. The 180th Brigade was chosen to make this attack for the Division (94–96).

In early October Mike Hogg's Houston friend Raymond Dickson, major of field artillery, made contact with him and wrote to Will that Mike had "a pretty bad ankle that he sprained on the last drive." But Mike Hogg was never one to complain.

[Co. D] After being relieved from the St. Mihiel sector, Company D was ordered to Domgermain, arriving on the afternoon of October 11th, after a strenuous hike. [This "hike" would not be the last one: Infantrymen carried eighty pounds of gear on their backs. The distance from St. Mihiel to the Meuse-Argonne front was eighty kilometers (fifty miles)]. Here the Company received replacements from the 84th Division, and on October 15th, were on their way to the front again. The Company arrived at Camp St. Pierre on the morning of October 18th, where it remained until October 22nd. The Brigade then moved forward, and took up its position in reserve of the 179th Brigade, which had taken Bantheville, and established a line on the high ground north of the town.[38]

From then until the November 11 armistice, as Mike's next letter says, he was indeed "on active service."

> *On Active Service with the*
> *American Expeditionary Force*
> *October 28, 1918*
> *My Birthday*
> *Dear Sis:*
> *My gas mask happens to be my writing desk at this writing. My old helmet lies at my feet and I am most covered with the "lamb's wool" comfort that you gave me. My <u>abode</u> is simply a fox-hole, with a little piece of canvas stretched over it.*
> *It has been some time since I wrote last—about a month, I should say. I cabled you, however, not long ago. Yes, I am at the front and that is the reason for the few between. I wish I could just tabulate what can be observed from this very spot. I'll tell you it would fill several pages.*
> *The boys are all in good spirits, and so is the weather, right now.*
> *I have been getting your mail quite regularly. I certainly appreciate it. Brother never writes. Once in a while, he drops me a line, or sends me a clipping. . . . We get papers dropped from aeroplanes and are able to keep up pretty well with what is going on. I have kept up, as have all of us, with the German Peace Offensive* [Germany's unsuccessful efforts to arrive at a cease-fire].[39] *We do not put much faith in it—in fact, none. We must whip these devils before anything else.*
> *Now, about that Christmas package. I don't know of anything I can use, except socks. The ones I have are great and come in fine. It seems to make no difference about the size. They all fit the foot very well.*
> *Give my regards to my friends but don't pass my letters around too much. This one is no good, so can't make the rounds.*
> *With bushels of love -*
> *Mike.*

Two days after his thirty-third birthday, Mike Hogg moved to the front lines again. This time he was heading into the great Battle of the Meuse-Argonne.

[Co. D] On the night of October 30th, the 180th Brigade relieved the 179th Brigade. . . . On the night of October 31st, Company

D moved into its position in the Bois-de-Bantheville, just a few hundred yards from the enemy.[40]

George Wythe explained the enormous significance of the Meuse-Argonne offensive on the Western Front:

[GW] While the St. Mihiel operation contained many elements that appeal to the imagination and probably will remain longer in the memory of the participants, and although it was the first great attack of the First American Army and was filled with all the eagerness and enthusiasm of the long-hoped-for American offensive, the battle of the Meuse-Argonne is much more important from a strategical standpoint. . . .

The battle of the Meuse-Argonne may be divided into three phases: Big advances were made on the first day, but after that the advance slowed down. The second phase began on October 4, when the army collected itself together, put in fresh troops, and at 5:30 a.m. attacked anew all along the line. No spectacular result was achieved. From that time on to November 1, individual divisions and corps were allowed to straighten out their lines and advance accordingly as the local situation would permit . . .

The third and last phase opened on November 1, when the army drove through to a decision (78–79). . . .

By this time the 179th Brigade was pretty well spent. Only eight officers remained in the 1st Battalion, 357th Infantry, and some companies were so badly reduced that it was necessary to consolidate them. October 31 proved to be "D minus one day"— that is, one day before the big attack.

The 180th Brigade, which was to deliver the attack, was brought into line the night of October 30–31, long enough before the attack to allow it to become familiar with the terrain. This policy proved to be doubly wise in view of the heavy artillery reaction the night before the attack, which reaction would have caught both brigades at the worst possible moment, when relieving and relieved troops are both in the forward zone. As it turned out, the relief was made without a casualty (96–98).

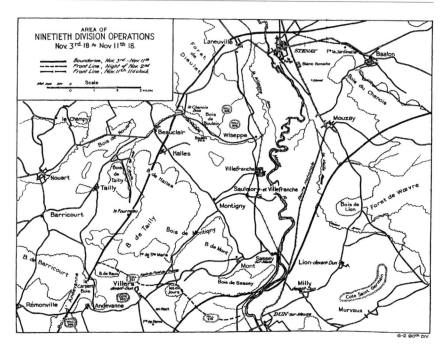

90th Division Operations, November 3–11, 1918. Source: Major George Wythe, *History of the 90th Division*, following p. 114.

But the 180th Brigade had already suffered many casualties, and was far from being at full strength.

[GW] When the 180th Brigade jumped off on November 1 its strength was only at 50 per cent of its officers and 65 per cent of its enlisted personnel. . . .

The principal feature on the immediate front of the Division was the wooded ridge running north along the left boundary— that is, roughly speaking, between Grand Carré Farm and the heights north of Andevanne. From this high ground there was an open slope toward the Meuse. . . . The highest point in the region was a hill known as Côte 243, which was just west of Villers-devant-Dun. . . .

As to the organization of the terrain by the enemy, suffice it to say that on November 1 the 90th Division held a line opposite the Freya Stellung [the Germans' last prepared line of defense].

This defensive position, which the Germans relied upon to hold the American attacks, was organized in depth to include a first or covering position between Aincreville and Grande Carré Farm, and, secondly, the main line of resistance, which embraced Andevanne, Côte 243, and Villers-devant-Dun. And it was manned with troops rated among the best in the German army. . . .

As the operations in the Meuse-Argonne region shaded into what is popularly known as "open warfare," as compared with "trench warfare" and "warfare of position," there was not to be found on this front the maze of trenches and entanglements, such as faced the Division at St. Mihiel. The artificial defenses consisted for the most part of pits for machine gunners and "foxholes." The latter are individual pits dug at scattered intervals so as to afford the maximum protection from shell fire. There was some wire, particularly on Côte 243, but the enemy relied principally upon machine guns, concealed in woods, holes, and isolated farms or villages, to bar the way (98–99).

On the morning of November 1st, at 3:30 a.m., the fiercest drive in which Company D took part, began with a barrage put over by the 155th Field Artillery, located in the valley in the rear, and the 343rd and the 345th Machine Gun Battalions, part of which was scattered along the front lines in the woods. A terrific barrage was kept up for two hours, which we later learned from the prisoners and wounded who came into our hands, was "most efficient." The Machine Gun Battalions in doing their part, fired over one million two hundred thousand rounds of ammunition. The Germans' counter barrage was by no means compared with ours. Their artillery was dropping shells in the valley just to the rear, and their machine guns were clipping the branches of trees overhead.

At 5:30 a.m., the Company moved out of its position in the woods, [every man] being out of the hole that he had dug only a few hours before. Passing single file for about two hundred yards along a winding trail that led through heavy undergrowth, the Company came out on the road along the Grande Carré Farm, about one hundred yards to the left of the farm buildings.[41]

[GW] H-hour was 5:30 a.m. No sooner had the assaulting wave debouched from its cover when a terrific machine gun fire poured into the lines. Particular trouble was experienced from the direction of Grande Carré Farm, which was well situated on the top of the open ridge. Despite the thoroughness of our magnificent artillery barrage, many enemy gunners found cover in the shelters in the vicinity of the farm and came to surface again in time

to catch the advancing infantry (102).

[Co. D] Fifty yards beyond the road, Company D, after meeting heavy resistance from machine gun fire, formed a skirmish line with the first platoon on the right, the fourth on the left, the third in the second wave, and the second platoon in reserve. Later it was found that the resistance consisted of eleven machine gun nests, located on the top of a small knoll one hundred to one hundred fifty yards beyond the road, some among trees and others in the open to the left. At this point we were held up for a short time until our right flank, under command of Sergt. Hulan F. Stanley, advanced to a position where they could get a closer field of fire and clean out the nests. It was here while directing his men that Sergt. Stanley received wounds which later resulted in death. The enemy having suffered heavy losses from the artillery barrage and the successful flank attack was forced to abandon their strong point. Those that remained, numbering seventy, came through our lines as prisoners. The Company suffered several casualties in this first encounter.

From this point it advanced about two kilometers [1.2 miles], northwest over open country, thence into a woods. While passing through the woods it advanced under shell fire.[42]

[GW] Lieutenant Fleming Burk, commanding Company D, which was maintaining liaison with the 89th Division, was wounded, Lieu-tenant Alfred L. Jones taking command in his stead (102).

[Co. D] Here, also, Company D lost its First Sergeant, Herbert W. Reed, and most of the runners. After leaving the woods and advancing through a small clearing, a second resistance was encountered in a small narrow woods on a side slope. The resistance was very slight as the enemy was withdrawing. Fifteen prisoners were taken, including two doctors found in an aid station.

After passing through the woods and advancing one hundred yards from the edge the Company came under heavy artillery and machine gun fire.[43]

[GW] At 8:30 a.m. an attempt was made to resume the advance, but the line was halted by a withering fire. Twice again a start forward was made, but the result was so ghastly that the line was halted, the men taking refuge in shell-holes. . . . Col. Price ordered the
2nd Battalion to take up the advance (102).

[Co. D] This barrage being so terrific and at point blank range, Company D was forced to retire to the woods. Due to its heavy losses and the open country furnishing no protection whatever to the advancing riflemen, a withdrawal was advisable in order to reorganize and attack from the flank. It was here that Sergt. Lewis Wiggins laid down his life while reconnoitering and directing his men to better positions.[44]

[GW] The 1st Battalion, which had moved forward to the right rear of the 2nd Battalion, was in position south of Andevanne at 4:30 p.m. when Major W. H. H. Morris, the commanding officer, received orders to pass to the right of the 2nd Battalion and seize Côte 243 (103).

[Co. D] During the afternoon the enemy withdrew, except a battery of 77's and a machine gun, which harassed Company D, which had then joined the First Battalion, 360th Infantry, and was advancing toward their new objective, Hill 243.[45]

[GW] Owing to the darkness it was necessary for the battalion to advance by compass bearing (104).

[Co. D] Company D formed with the Battalion in line of combat groups and their cover of darkness moved forward, into enemy lines, approximately three kilometers [1.8 miles].[46]

[GW] Shells from our own artillery, which had been playing on the hill at intervals throughout the day, were bursting on Côte 243 when Major Morris reached the foot of the wooded heights. As telephonic communication with regimental headquarters had been maintained practically continuously, the artillery fire was soon stopped and the battalion moved up the hill. Major Morris established his P. C. [command post] there about 8:00 p.m. Captain Gustav Dittmar, Captain Mike Hogg, Lieutenant Lonus Read, and Lieutenant Robert Campbell were wounded during the advance (104).

Mike Hogg's wound was not severe. He was hit in the neck by a shell fragment and taken to a military hospital for treatment. A brief note to Will Hogg from the Office of the US Adjutant General informed him that Captain Hogg was "slightly wounded and in Service of Supply Hospital about November 6th. He has doubtless communicated with you, either from hospital or since return to duty."[47] If Mike did send immediate word about being wounded, his letter has not survived. He took his wound lightly. In a letter to Will in February 1919 he described his injury as "nothing at all." Apparently he did not write of it to Ima. And he was back in command of Company D, 1st Battalion, 360th Infantry, 180th Brigade, soon after November 6.

[Co. D] Arriving at the objective Hill 243, which was taken without resistance, a patrol was sent out to reconnoiter positions. The patrol soon learned that Company D was camped within the enemy battery positions. During the night the patrol came into contact with a detachment of the enemy that was endeavoring to move their field pieces from this position. Evidently none of the enemy detachment escaped, for the next day a reinforcement of the enemy attempted the same performance and were driven off by Company A, Company D, having taken up their position along a narrow gauge railroad track facing Hill 321.

The task of capturing Hill 321 was by no means an easy one, we soon learned. After a short artillery preparation the Company went "Over the Top" at 12:03 p.m., through a heavy artillery and the fiercest machine gun barrage imaginable. (The Company at this time was in liaison between Company A, First Battalion, and Company I, of the Second Battalion.) After more than three hours of the most stubborn fighting, the Company succeeded in establishing its position on the crest of the Hill. The enemy having been reinforced, came back with a strong counter attack. This attack was likewise repulsed, and the remainder of the night was spent without events, except the task of carrying the wounded from the field, which lasted well into the morning.[48]

[GW]The big attack had been a complete success. By 4:30 p.m.—the hour that the 2nd Battalion, 360th Infantry, had achieved its mission for the day—all troops of the 180th Brigade were on the corps objective, thus breaking the Freya Stellung. . . . The enemy's main line of resistance was broken (105).

[Co. D] But the enemy was far from defeated. The next day, November 2, saw "severe machine gun opposition all along the division front," as the Germans used machine gun nests to cover their withdrawal. . . .

Company D, having been relieved, marched back to Andevanne, where we were to receive our first hot meal for many days and probably a dry place to sleep. With the rapid advance of the first line it became necessary to move forward again, and the Company remained at Andevanne only long enough to satisfy their craving stomachs. Immediately after dark it moved forward in a drenching rain, trudging wearily over the shell plowed fields and after a few hours came to a small woods opposite the St. Mare Farm, where it stayed for the night.

The following morning, the march was resumed into the Bois-de-Tally, about one kilometer away, where the men dug "fox holes" and prepared for a short stay. After four days in this position the Company was ordered to Villers-devant-Dun, where it remained until November 10th.[49]

[GW]The period from the time our victorious battalions reached the bluffs overlooking the Meuse River on November 3 until definite orders were received on November 9 to make a crossing and take up the pursuit, was one of great uncertainty (114).

From November 3 to 11 the troops were never out of German artillery range.[50]

[GW]The physical condition of the men of the 360th Infantry was very serious at this time. The physical strain of the severe fighting in piercing the Freya Stellung; the damp, unhealthy surroundings in which they found themselves in the Bois de Montigny, without sufficient blankets or overcoats, as all packs had not yet been brought up; impure water and cold meals at uncertain hours—these were some of the circumstances which made nearly forty per cent. of the regiment victims of diarrhea, and twenty per cent. patients with sub-acute bronchitis. In view of these conditions, it was decided to put the men in better billets. The morning of November 7 they marched to billets as follows: Regimental P. C. and 3d Battalion, Andevanne; 1st Battalion, Villers-devant-Dun; and 2d Battalion, Bantheville (119). . . .

The news of the abdication of the Kaiser [on November 9] came at the moment that the Meuse was being crossed. In a despatch from Berlin, the Imperial Chancellor, Prince Max of Baden, published the statement: "The Emperor and King has decided to abdicate the throne."

The end of hostilities was now plainly in sight. Since the signing of the armistice with Bulgaria on October 29, with Turkey on October 31, and with Austria-Hungary on November 4, the days of further fighting had been numbered. The hope for peace, however, did not in any way slow down the offensive. Rather, it was the universal desire to fight all the harder in order to deliver the knock-out blow as soon as possible.

Through the radio despatches sent out from the Eiffel Tower in Paris, picked up by division, brigade and regimental radio sets, the progress of the armistice negotiations was followed with interest (123).

[Co. D] At 4:00 a.m., November 10th Company D was again on its way to the front lines, passing through the town of Mouzay, which was being shelled by the Germans, it came out on the road to the north of the town. The Company was then under observation, however, the advance was continued. The enemy did their best to stop the progress with high explosive and much gas. At 8:30 p.m., the Company had reached its new position just a few hundred yards from the town of Baalon. (Distance marched twenty-two kilometers [about 13.5 miles].)[51]

[GW] The fighting on the day preceding the armistice was both severe and costly. It is probable that no other division in the Expeditionary Forces met with such stubborn resistance during the last hours preceding the cessation of hostilities. According to prisoners' statements, the next German position behind the Meuse was along the heights north and east of the Chiers River, which runs through Montmédy. But the retirement to this position was by no means precipitate. In order to cover this withdrawal, the enemy had left two companies out of each regiment, on the heights between Stenay and Baalon and in the Bois du Chenois, southwest of Baalon, and this force fought with the fiendish skill which characterized German rear-guards. . . .

The casualties in our ranks on November 10 testify to the nature of the operations, one officer and 33 enlisted men being killed, and 12 officers and 171 men wounded (123–124).

[Co. D] During the Meuse-Argonne operation Company D had nineteen men killed, fifty four wounded and one missing.[52]

As terrible as this war's death toll was, it was not as large as it was in three earlier American wars. In the Mexican War (1846–1848) the death rate from diseases and wounds for each year per thousand men was 110; in the Civil War, 65; in the Spanish-American War, 26. In World War I, the rate was 19.[53]

[GW] The Division had given the order to the 179th Brigade to hold the ground it had captured, with the intention of passing through the 180th Brigade, which was to renew the attack at daybreak in the direction of Montmédy. This order was issued about eleven o'clock on the night of the 10th. Further orders from the 3d Army Corps changed the zone of action of the 90th Division, and assigned the national highway from Stenay to Montmédy to the 89th Division, on our left. Still later in the night, at about 1 a.m., it was necessary to make still further changes.

Field Order No. 21, 90th Division, as finally issued, explained the plans for November 11 as follows: The first mission of the Division would be to assist the 89th Division in crossing the Meuse at Pouilly and by pontoon bridges between Inor and Stenay. This mission was to be carried out by the 179th Brigade by pressing the enemy and seizing any ground possible between Stenay and Baalon. The 89th Division was to attack at daybreak and capture the heights east and southeast of Inor. When it had succeeded in this task, the second mission of the 90th Division would be undertaken, namely, to advance in liaison with the 89th Division against the heights overlooking the Chiers River.

The 180th Brigade was to perform this second mission. It moved up before daylight of the 11th, in readiness to advance when the time came (128).

There was no let up in the fighting, as General Pershing wrote later: "By November 10 the infantry had crossed the Meuse and the town of Mouzay was taken. The division was pressing the enemy hard at the time of the signing of the armistice."[54]

[GW] The glad tidings that the armistice was signed were received at division headquarters at 7:20 a.m. The following bulletin from the 3d Army Corps was published:

"1. You are informed that hostilities will cease along the whole front at 11 hours on November 11, 1918, Paris time.

"2. No allied troops will pass the line reached by them at that hour and date until further orders.

"3. All communication with the enemy, both before and after the termination of hostilities, is absolutely forbidden. In case of violation of this order the severest disciplinary measures will be immediately taken. Any officer offending will be sent to these headquarters under guard.

"4. Every emphasis will be laid on the fact that the arrangement is an armistice only, and not a peace.

"5. There must not be the slightest relaxation of vigilance. The troops must be prepared any moment for further operations. Special steps will be taken by all commanders to insure the strictest discipline and that all troops are in readiness and fully prepared for any eventualities. Division and brigade commanders and commanders of corps units will personally inspect all organizations with the foregoing in view" (129–130).

Somewhere in France or Belgium
November 14th, 1918
Dear Sis:

I am now only a few kilometers from where I was when we got the almost unbelievable news that there was to be a suspension of all hostilities at eleven o'clock. The Germans were only a few yards away and we were preparing to make a <u>desperate</u> *attack that morning. I had already given up all idea of coming through. You should have seen the place where we spent the night—and such a night! Everybody and everything was frozen stiff.*

We got the news at about ten-thirty. There was absolutely no demonstration. We could not make a sign or move, because of danger. Shells were still falling. At eleven, we heard the German bugles blow and the men shout. We then saw them get right up from in front of us and "beat it" back. All firing ceased. MY! But it was great. We were too tired and chilled, though, to realize what great luck we and the world in general were in. We have been through a great deal of fighting and I suppose are very lucky.

[GW] The news that the "war is over" was received without excitement. The men of the 1st Battalion, 360th Infantry, who were set for another scrap, were almost disappointed. They sighed, and dug in a little deeper, for "you never can tell" (130).

Mike's letter of November 14, continued:

Raymond came around in his <u>car</u> today, and we had a long and wonderful ride over the great battlefield. I took him to the very spot where my company and myself were waiting through the night to "jump off" in the morning.

He can tell you about my abode that night. Raymond looks fine and is doing splendidly. He and I are going into the rest business when we get home. I tell him that he must come and live with us and he has about consented.

Lieutenant Jones is still with me. He has proven to be a very brave and great soldier.

You should see the town we are in. It is in better shape than most any around here and, at that, there is not a single house left whole. I am in one of the best and it has three rooms left. They are only baby rooms. I have a warm fire, just the same, and so have the men. We have all had a <u>bath</u> and have on warm and clean clothes—always get hot and good food after a fight.

[GW] Notwithstanding the signing of the armistice, the Division remained prepared for any eventualities, and continued to hold the outpost lines established at 11 a.m., November 11. However, immediate steps were taken to place as many men as possible in comfortable billets, to bring up officers' bedding rolls and men's packs which had been left behind in the fighting, and to provide baths and new clothes and equipment (177).

Mike's November 14 letter to Ima, continued:

Sis, if she had not been over the day she was, you would have been minus one young brother. You know, there is a limit to everything, and I had reached mine. I hope Raymond will get a wire home long before this reaches you.

No, I have not written very often, because it has been impossible to write at times. I have been on the front for almost four months and in places where it was not healthy to do any writing. However, I think you have missed getting some of my letters. I have written at least once every two weeks at all times.

Here is just an enumeration of things which I saw one day while we were on a hill in reserve, on the night we went up to relieve another outfit:

A marsh just below the hill, full of dead horses, torn-up wagons, and cannon. A road just beyond the marsh, winding up a hill in one direction to where a town once stood, but now nothing but white bricks mark the place—in the other direction, the road stretched as far as the eye could see over almost level country. From the top of the hill to as far as could be seen, the road was chucked and blocked with trucks, troops, cannon, horses, ration and munition trains.

All along the slope of the hill where I was, torn helmets of Americans and Germans. Fresh American and German graves, old French graves, pieces of rifles, shreds of uniforms, packs, shoes, grenades, small holes in the ground all over the side of the hill where men had dug in.

A railroad track, just this side of the marsh, all torn to pieces. Old pieces of machine guns and ammunition belts of Germans, where they had tried to make a stand.

The top of the hill all around me covered with what used to be brush, but which was now chewed up by machine gun bullets and looked as if rats had been eating it. Three large observation balloons, one of which was brought down by a Boche. The air alive with aeroplanes. Some were throwing propaganda, which looked like snow falling.

Shells falling and knocking up the earth every few minutes. Our boys sticking close to the ground; cook stoves camouflaged and in full blast. Every hill in sight full of American Infantry or Artillery soldiers; litter-bearers going after someone just hit by a piece of shell.

These are a few of the things I saw from that one spot. Imagine what could be seen when on the move.

Mike Hogg and his comrades had indeed been "on the move." The 90th Division had been "under fire from August 20 to November 11, with the exception of several days consumed in changing sectors, for a total of 75 days."[55]

[GW] The terms of the Armistice had provided that the Germans should turn over to the Allies specified amounts of war materials. In order to receive this surrendered property detachments of the 90th Division were ordered on November 16 to Longuyon and on November 17 to Virton (Belgium). The 1st Battalion of the 358th Infantry and the 358th Machine Gun Company marched to Longuyon under command of Lieutenant-Colonel James W. Everington, and upon arrival there inventoried and established guards over a large number of cannon, machine guns, bombing planes, and locomotives. The 1st Battalion, 360th Infantry, and the 360th Machine Gun Company were trucked to Virton under command of Major William H. H. Morris (177–178).

Somewhere in France
November 23, 1918 (Saturday)
Dear Sis:

I feel like I imagine an old bear feels when he has been hibernating all winter and has just crawled out of his hole. We are in a city. The sun is shining. I have a nice room—electric lights and a bath. There are no screaming shells, no boggy ditches, frozen blankets, no attacks to be made just before day, etc., and so on. The men are all comfortably quartered, have new, beautiful clothes, look the picture of ruddy health, and drill with great spirit. There are real, live, happy people about— and even dogs and chickens. It is great to hear the dogs howling and barking at night!

Nothing but beautiful weather since the armistice. Isn't that strange? Before, it was nothing but rain—night and day. It is cold all right—ice everywhere.

We had the experience of being the first Allied troops in this place. A regiment of Germans left just as we entered. Our welcome was one never to be forgotten. The inhabitants could not believe their own eyes. It took them almost a day to become assured that all was well—then such demonstrations!

They must have had their flags buried during the war. Anyway, you never saw the like of Belgian, French and American flags. They covered the earth. The celebrations are not over yet. Every night, they have a new cause for parading, dancing and speaking. They give all credit to the Americans.

The people here are a clean lot. They average up much better than I have seen in other places. No one seems to show any signs of starvation, either.

I am sure that what we have before us will be very interesting, but, for the first time, we are all having home uppermost in our minds. The spirit of the boys is wonderful. They show the proper attention in everything. They will carry this business through as they did the <u>livelier</u> one, or deadlier, I should say, but really they, I fear, will have a harder time, on account of having so much time to think of home.

I can't even guess when we will be leaving for America. I am glad enough that the war is over and hope some day to be home. The sooner, the better.

With much love -
Mike.

[GW] The citizens of the recaptured villages had many tales to tell of their hardships during the four years of German occupation. Meat had been unknown since the entry of America into the war cut off the supply previously received through the Belgian Relief Commission.[56] Eggs were taken by the Germans for their own use. Letter-writing to relatives in France was forbidden. Their expressions of joy for their deliverance by the Americans knew no bounds, and at Mouzay, on the steps of the city hall, in the presence of all the assembled citizenry, General Allen was presented with a bouquet of flowers and an American flag (179).

The armies of the Allies moved toward the Rhine simultaneously, following up the withdrawing German forces. The sectors from Holland to Switzerland were originally allotted as follows: Belgians, British, French, Americans, then French again. The Belgians were on the extreme north and were to occupy Brussels, later Liège, and then the left bank of the Rhine opposite Dusseldorf. Adjoining them on the south were the British, who advanced in the direction of Namur, Spa, Malmédy, to the bridgehead at Cologne. The French armies, which came next, had a wedge-shaped sector which came to a point at the line which had been the German frontier before the war. This wedge was through the heart of the Ardennes, with Bastogne in the center. The axis of march of the American army was through Luxemburg and thence along the valley of the Moselle River (180). . . .

The route followed was an extremely interesting one. In the reclaimed towns of France our troops were received with the greatest enthusiasm. Towns were decorated with flowers and greenery; banners bore words of greeting; and at gatherings of all the citizenry, commanders were presented with bouquets and flowers. The Americans were acclaimed as deliverers. In the little town of Epiez the town council changed the name of the principal street to "Rue President Wilson," and of another street to "Rue General O'Neil," in honor of the division commander (184).

December 5, 1918

Dear Sis:

We did not stay but a few days in Virton, Belgium. That was the place where we were the first Allies to enter. We certainly hated to leave. You have, no doubt, read descriptions of the thousands of prisoners swarming out of Germany. A great many of them came our way, and I can vouch for the accuracy of what I have read in some of the papers.

For several days, now, we have been marching through Luxembourg. The people here are, of course, almost all German, however, we are treated as nicely as could be hoped for anywhere. They are all fine. Right now, we are at Remich, a half-German and Luxembourg city. It is on the border and on the Moselle River. We understand that we will have friendly treatment all the way to the Rhine.

Speaking of hiking, I thought we had hiked before, but I was mistaken. That is about all we do now. Every day, all day long, we "hit the road." At first, it was rather hard, but we are getting used to it now. I have not lost a single man from the Company since we started.

We have several weeks more before us and then, I think, we are through for a while.

It is hard to write and still harder to mail a letter these days. When we halt, we are not only tired out, but there is no place to mail letters. I am standing the pace better than most of the men.

I was absolutely exhausted for a week or two after the Armistice. I did not realize how completely I was gone till I got to feeling <u>right</u>. I went to bed and stayed there for over a week and never ate anything but oatmeal or milk-toast. The treatment was great.

It seems to me that it will be some time yet before we will begin to go home. Since I feel so fine, I think that I will not mind a bit, but will rather like the new experiences. However, the sensation of having experiences has gotten to be rather old, and not so much to one's liking.

Yes, the 90th is one of the very "top notchers." We have gotten great citations from all who command us. There were only a few divisions over there that saw more real fighting than we did. We were in the line for several months, on the most active fronts, with no relief.

Colonel Price is still in command of our Regiment. The 360th has a most enviable record. We have done more than was expected on every fighting occasion and, strange to say, the 1st Battalion has done twice as much of the fighting as any Battalion in the Regiment. We have a young West Point major [Major William H. H. Morris Jr.], whom all concede to be the most brilliant soldier they have seen. You should see him in the field. I think there is no one like him.

With much love -
Mike.

On November 14, 1918, Major General Henry T. Allen issued General Order No. 144, which said, in part:

> The division commander has no adequate words to express his great satisfaction and delight with the fine military spirit of the division, and his pride in its fighting value after seventy-four days (less an interval of seven days) in the fighting lines. . . . In spite of the severe losses and terrific demands that these successes have exacted, the indomitable spirit, and keenness to fight continue to characterize the division. Every member of this gallant force has a right to be proud of the services he has rendered in a great cause of human liberty. Our country may count with assurance upon the execution with success of whatever duty it may entrust of the 90th Division.[57]

Captain Mike Hogg received another document, which he sent home. It sums up his, and the 180th Brigade's, military record in the war.

HEADQUARTERS 180TH INFANTRY BRIGADE
   Nov. 24, 1918
   MEMORANDUM:
   To Officers and Men of the Texas Brigade:
   In his farewell letter to you on Nov. 21, 1918, the Division Commander gave you the highest possible praise for soldierly qualities. He had already told you that the Commanding General, First US Army had recently stated to the Commander-in-Chief that "The 90th Division is as good as **** Divisions; you have not a better Division; it is as good and dependable as any Division in the Army." Higher commendation could not be bestowed. In order that you may know some of the reasons for such unstinted praise, I will recount some of your deeds:

   On September 12th you had your first fight and broke through those bewildering mazes of wire and entrenchments called the Quarter-Reserve and the Western end of the notorious Bois-le-Prêtre. In defending the Southern portion of this wood, the French are reported to have lost one hundred twenty-three thousand men, of whom eighteen thousand were killed. The whole Bois-le-Prêtre was cleared in a neat operation by the 360th Infantry, on September 13th, with slight loss—the exploitation being carried to the Moselle River.

   You advanced your lines close up to Prény and Pagny-sur-Moselle and took part in the general demonstration made along the whole battle-front from the Moselle to the Channel, on September 26th. You were relieved on the night of October 9–10, to go to the Meuse-Argonne Front. . . .

   On October 23, you were on the Meuse-Argonne front and it fell to your lot to wage the attack on the Freya Stellung for the Division on November 1st and 2nd and your exploitation carried you from Dun-sur-Meuse to near the Tuileries farm, on a front of seven kilometers [about 4.3 miles]. This Freya Stellung was the last organized German defense line and, where it reached the Meuse, was the pivot or hinge on which swung the whole defensive system through Northern France and Belgium.

   Here at Andevanne and Villers-devant-Dun, on a front of four kilometers [about 2.5 miles], by a superb assault that has not been excelled in this war for nicety of execution or for ferocity of action, you smashed the defensive system at its hinges.

This imperiled the whole German Army; then came the clamor for an armistice and the collapse of the war. . . .

The names Bois des Rappes, Bois de Bantheville, Le Grande Carré, Andevanne, Côte 243, Côte 321, and Villers-devant-Dun are branded upon your memories. The Machine Gun Companies will not forget that they fired one million one hundred fifty thousand rounds during November 1st and 2nd.

Here is a proud boast for this brigade—not a soldier straggled from his regiment.

You were always facing the enemy and on the night before the armistice took effect, you were formed up facing him, ready to deliver another mighty blow at daylight of that fateful morning of November 11th.

You have shared equally with the best and have deserved everything.

You are soldiers, and I am proud of you.

(Signed) U. G. McAlexander,

Brigadier General[58]

Meanwhile, the 90th Division was now part of the Army of Occupation.[59]

[GW] The foremost troops of the Allies had crossed the German frontier on Sunday, December 1 but the 90th Division did not reach this line until nearly a week later. The 180th Brigade crossed the Moselle River over the bridge at Remich and entered German territory on December 6. On the following day the 179th Brigade, less the 357th Infantry, crossed the Sauer River, the boundary line between Luxembourg and Germany, at Wasserbillig. The 357th Infantry crossed at Grevenmacher. There was little indication that this was the land of the enemy. However, advance billeting parties were required to carry arms while engaged in their duties, and trucks were not allowed to move except in convoys of sufficient size to be able to defend themselves if attacked. It was soon seen that these precautions were unnecessary. German officials were almost servile in their desire to please the new rulers, and the inhabitants were either obediently indifferent or profuse in their desire to satisfy the wants of the occupying troops (184–186).

. . . .

Tuesday, December 18th

Dear Sis:

This is the first time in some time that I have even had a chance to draw a breath. Hike! Hike! Hike!—it has been for weeks. Day in and day out we march. It has all been very interesting, though. I think when I get back home, I can tell you anything you want to know about any part of the Moselle. We followed its banks to within about thirty miles of the Rhine.

We then turned west and are now located at Dann, a very pretty town about the same distance from the Rhine. I should not have said <u>located</u> because we got here last night and leave again tomorrow. We are lucky to get this "lay-over."

We have had absolutely no trouble with the Germans. They are a strange lot to me. They treat us as though we are their long lost friends, instead of their enemies, but we do not trust them. Continually, they try to spread all kinds of rumors.

This country does not seem to me to be in such bad shape. We see more feed here than we did in France. The country looks a thousand times better. Every foot of ground which can be cultivated is being used. Even the vineyards[,] which grow way up on the sides of the mountains, are not being in the least neglected.

This march keeps us completely out of touch with the world. We know nothing and hear less.

This regiment has made a wonderful record throughout the march. I am sure none could be better. There are many regulations and we, to a man, comply with them. You know "hiking" for days is no easy job—in fact, it is the hardest I have yet found. Nevertheless, the men are coming through in fine spirits and in wonderful shape.

The scenery has at all times been beautiful. These mountains, with their many colors, beautiful villages, and <u>trained</u> forests, are always good for sore eyes, particularly if one has been where we have.

I am afraid I am getting a taste for good wine. The French may have good wine, but I have yet got to taste any that touches what we get here. Every night, I always have a good room in a fine home and nearly always, the people have something to eat and some wine. The men are not as lucky as the officers. Sometimes they sleep in barns (with good hay) and then again they get rooms. They always have plenty to eat. I have been hoping we would stop long enough somewhere to prepare a Christmas dinner for the men, but I have given up hope. No doubt, we will be on the road that day.

It has been really warm for the last two weeks. It rains all the time, but the days remind one of late Spring. They all say that any time now we are likely to have heavy snow. I certainly hope not.

Carter wrote me about his young daughter. Sure am sorry it is not a boy. I think Carter is, too.

I am enclosing a letter that I wrote some time ago but which until now I have not had a chance to mail. I hope I will be lucky enough to be able to write you within a week.

It looks as though there will not be an opportunity for time to drag. The program set for us is just as strenuous as ever. I expect to get about a hundred and thirty-five new men to fill up with soon. You have an idea what that means—Drill, drill, drill!

Oh, this is a great and <u>uncertain</u> life. We never know from one day to another where or what we will be the next.

With much love -
Mike.

Mike wrote a letter congratulating Houston friends on the birth of their daughter and describing his feelings on the day of the Armistice:

December 19, 1918
Dear Carter and Lelia:
When I was a kid, I often wished that I was a girl, so that when I grew up, I wouldn't have to go to war. That was when I was quite small—before the years rolled by and I became wise—<u>very wise</u>. Now that I have "rounded off" (I should say torn off) those selfsame years, and am again passing into childhood's blissful fancy, my imagination once more pictures the impossible—WAR—and I am glad we have a <u>new</u> Rebekah in our midst, instead of a young Carter or a fool "Mickey."

Rebekah and I are going to have great times on her birthdays—for two reasons. First, because it is her birthday; and second, because all of *my flesh, or most of it, was still on my bones that never-to-be-forgotten morning. There were only four line officers of the fourteen of our Battalion who were not either killed or severely wounded. One of the four [Hogg himself] was slightly wounded. He got hit in the neck just under the jaw with a shell fragment. Bleeding was profuse, but the wound slight and the <u>fool</u> lucky. This was the second morning of our attack on the Germans along the Meuse River and the day my Battalion went "over the top." German Machine-guns and artillery were never more deadly. Don't worry—we "mopped" up with them, anyway.*

Say, Fitz, the eleventh day of the eleventh month and the eleventh hour of that outfit was <u>something else</u>, too. We were all set to "hit" the Boche that morning when the word came down to hold and not "go over." We were only a short distance from each other and they had the commanding position, with lots of machine guns and artillery. My Company had dwindled from two [hundred] thirty-five men to sixty-five. We were all tired out, as well as frozen stiff. My limit was reached. I am sure, had we gone over that morning, my identification tags would have come in quite handy. Well, when we were informed that the Armistice was on, we were like a bunch of hoot owls that had just been suddenly taken from the dark into the light.

We are now seeing the Moselle Valley. No, we are not doing it by train or motor. It is a new experience to me—this tour de luxe on foot. Nearly since the beginning of the Armistice, we have been hiking every day. Many miles have we gone.

The marching has been great in many ways. We have seen most beautiful country. Our strength has been improved. The men have changed from pale to ruddy complexions, and are the picture of health; and our one-night stands have given us a very good insight into German life. We hope soon to reach our permanent area somewhere on the Rhine.

You should see my billets on these nights. If it <u>is</u> only till five a.m., I am living in great style. Always one of the best homes in the town, where there are plenty of fine homes, falls to my lot. These people do everything for you. I don't consider the source, nor can I figure the idea, but it is much better than having to <u>TAKE</u> things, or be made to feel uncomfortable by a show of hostility.

I am anxious to get back and once more be a civilian—as Carter says, "A mere civilian."

Here's hoping that before many months, we will all __FOUR__ be together.
Please remember me to the grandparents.
As ever,
Mike.

December 24, 1918
Dear Brother and Sister:
I wrote the greater part of this young note at dawn, some thirty-two miles from here. I am now at Wehlen, a beautiful little town on the Moselle River. This is our Christmas present. We have, at last, reached our permanent home, after marching since the twenty-eighth of last month. We have been north of here, almost to the Rhine. We arrived here last night. The hike was about thirty kilometers [about 18.6 miles] and could not have been more beautiful. We came from the west and, before we could get to the Moselle Valley, had to go up and up. The scenery was most beautiful when we reached the crest of the mountains overlooking the Moselle and its deep valley. It was so far below that it seemed hopeless to ever get there. It was, too. It took nearly two hours to wind our way down to it.

The men all have good beds, the town is clean, the scenery cannot be beat anywhere, the people make everything yours, and we are assured that this is our place of occupation—best of all! Just think! We have been no place for longer than a week since August the 18th, except when we were in a "drive." It is a great Christmas present!

You should see this desk that I am writing on. I am living in the home of a rich wine-merchant. These people are all wine dealers and are all surprisingly well-to-do. Going back to the desk: It is a real one, like the very best you find at home. This large, beautiful room serves me as a lounging, reading and dining room. There are a library, German and American magazines, this desk, a beautiful sideboard—not bare, but laden with china, cut-glass, silverware and, on top, some huge steins—a big divan sits before a large fireplace and, not far off is a chair, built on the order of those things which sit on the porch at the Varner. Sister should see the clock—it is a dream. She would also be interested in the curtains, etc. but we are not. The kitchen!—it opens into this room. It is modern and German. You know what that means— everything there that one needs. My room is across the hall—as nice as anyone could have.

I have a wonderful cook. He takes this army "chow" and camouflages it till you think you are at some real, live restaurant. We get stuff, though, which does not require much of this. Good beef, flour, potatoes, corn meal, white bread, canned goods, fresh turnips, greens, lettuce, jams, etc.

I see that I neglected to tell you that the kitchen and dining room, with everything in them, are used solely by me. The officers of my Company are, of course, a part of me. These people offered it and seem glad to have us use everything. Things that we overlook, they bring to our attention. This is the attitude of the whole of them. The Americans, for their part, are keeping on their side of the fence, and are dealing, at all times in a fair and decent manner.

It seems that we have changed from a fighting army to a "hiking" organization. We have been "hiking" and parading over German territory and through German cities and villages almost since the Armistice.

[GW] The period from the time that the 90th Division took up the march on November 24 until December 21, when Division Headquarters were established at Bemcastel, Germany, was one of almost daily marches. The marches were conducted practically the same as under peace-time conditions. While all units put out advance-guards and observed all precautions for security, the dispositions seemed more like training maneuvers than an advance into the enemy's country. The strictest march discipline was enforced, and great stress was laid on the correct formation of the column and the appearance of the men and transport. Each regiment had a uniform style of pack, and the organizations vied with each other in their attempts to present the smartest set-up (182).

Mike's letter of December 24, continued:

The following details, which are most strictly observed, down to the last "bone-head" in the Company, or someone catches Hell—me—will give you a slight idea of how we appear and what a really creditable showing the troops are making, as they weave their way "up stream and down," meaning, over hills and down valleys on fair roads, while rain constantly keeps one reminded that these roads are sometimes turned into small rivers: Well, anyway, here are a few things that we are minutely checked on by some "hard-boiled" Inspector, whose whole job depends on how many irregularities he can detect. He is to be found at every crook and turn. Men will make the "short pack." The bottom of the roll will be not more than two inches below the last strap. Overcoats, when not worn, will be rolled so that the T.O. [the 90th Division's insignia was a red T intersecting an O, for the Texas and Oklahoma Brigades] *is to the left and is plainly visible; the collar must be turned in, the coat rolled as tightly as possible, and tied with four leather strings. Slickers, when not needed, will be rolled over the overcoat—leather jerkins carried inside overcoat roll. These rolls will be lashed over the haversack; helmets will be worn, and must be kept greased at all times. The "chin strap" will be worn on point of chin. Gas masks will be worn at the "alert." The muzzle of the gun will, at all times, be carried up. When passing through towns, the "piece" will be carried at right shoulder and troops at attention. The band will play through all towns. Litters will be carried at rear of column; men will keep step at all times. There will be forty inches distance between men in formation column of twos. Men must keep covered off; fifteen paces between platoons, twenty-five between companies, one hundred between battalions, and there must always be an advance guard and march outpost. Troops will march fifty minutes and rest ten. Halts will be made ten minutes before the hour. No one will eat or drink till the noon halt—twenty minutes. All trash left from lunch will be gathered up and burned. Straggling will not be tolerated—any soldier falling out must have a written order from Company C.O. Failure to have said order will be a cause for charges against C.O. Troops will march on right of road. Battalion and Company C.O.'s will inspect their units each morning before the march. After the first, third, and last halts, all unit C.O.'s will step to side of road and inspect their unit as it passes. Troops, on reaching their billets, will not be allowed on the street until they and all their equipment has been "policed." "Call to Arms" may be expected at any time, night or day; Company punishment for those who appear not properly "policed."*

The men take all of these regulations most cheerfully and it goes as a part of the game. You would be surprised how few of them ever are found delinquent even in a detail. Also, organization after organization will pass a very rigid inspector and he will have virtually no criticism to make. Straggling and falling out are almost unknown. A man will almost die on his feet before he will fall out on the march. You see "guts"—real "guts"—shown every day. Several times, when we were where we could not get shoes, I have seen men march in with bleeding feet; without one thought of leaving the ranks.

The 90th Division has made a splendid record in all phases of its existence over here. This regiment stands out as by far the best of the 90th and we are, of course, very proud of it. We have lost many men—I should say at least sixty-five or seventy percent. That shows what fighting we have done. My company, the largest in the battalion, has one hundred and fifteen men. Some of these, quite a number, have returned from cured wounds. I had, at one time, two hundred and fifty.

Well, I will be glad when this whole thing is over and I can get in my old loos [sic] clothes. Two years of constant hard work have made me quite familiar with what it takes to make a fighting organization. I think I am proficient along that line. My outfit has been a success from the start, however, there are phases of the work which I dislike so much that only another war can induce me to become sufficiently interested to keep in touch with army life.

It seems strange that so short a time should put the "horrors of war" so far behind one. They have passed, to a great extent, from my mind, but not to such an extent that I would not do everything in my power to prevent another.

With love -
Mike.

January 12, 1919
Dear Sis:

There are absolutely no facilities for sending cables here. The only way we can ever send one is to be lucky enough to find someone who is going to Paris, or some other large city. It takes a cablegram nearly as long to reach here as a letter. I got your cablegram about two weeks after it was sent. You see, we are cut off from the outside world nearly as much as we have ever been.

Leaves are coming soon and I am expecting to get my week before long. Colonel Price and I are going together. We shall, of course visit Nice, etc. I have had no leave since I went to Camp Travis.

Our work now is not a bit interesting. It is the same old routine every day—drill, drill, drill. We are all happy, though, that it is no worse than that, and we manage to get along in a fine way.

You would never guess that things here were ever disturbed. There has been nothing to disturb the peace or quietness of our stay. The people are as humble as you please, and still continue to put themselves out for the Americans. Their civil life is allowed to go on in its normal manner.

We are having a series of Regimental and Divisional shows now. I have never seen a Majestic or Keith's which was better. Most all the performers are old-time professionals.

I am dumbfounded at the weather here. It has been warm, with the exception of just a few days. It rains, though, every day.

We hear all kinds of rumors about going home. There is a new story every day. To tell you the truth, I just missed going the other day. All officers in the Regiment who were in my class, except myself and one other, were ordered home. We are now getting it that we will be in the next order. It is expected out next week. Too good to be true. . . .

My, but we are in good shape. All are growing fatter every day. I will soon be up to my old standard, if I am not already there. I got a cable from brother the other day. He must think my health is bad. I answered him at my first opportunity and, among other things, said I was <u>sober.</u> Hope he got it.

Will see you by next fall, anyway.

With love -

Mike.

[GW] As G. H. Q. adopted a very liberal policy in granting leaves after the armistice, every officer and man had an opportunity to see some parts of France other than the battle zones before returning to the United States. The most popular leave area for the officers was the Riviera, while the majority of the enlisted men were sent to the Savoie area, near the Swiss border. In addition to the regular leave period every four months, shorter leaves to visit Paris for three days and to take boat rides up the Rhine from Coblenz were allotted very generously (194).

By February 1919 seven-day furloughs were available for leave time in France. Special trains carried up to 1,200 American soldiers a day to vacation in areas such as the French Riviera. Mike Hogg was soon among them. He was already thinking of coming home and hoping a longtime family friend might help speed his departure. Colonel

Edward M. House, a wealthy Texan and special foreign policy adviser to President Woodrow Wilson, was then in France. House had helped Mike's father, the late James Stephen Hogg, win the governorship of Texas in the 1890s, and the Hogg and House families had become good friends when they lived in Austin.[60]

> *Sunday, February 16, 1919*
> *Dear Brother:*
> *I have just returned from my two weeks leave. It is certainly a peculiar institution. I say institution because it is truly that. Everyone who takes advantage of one has the same experience.*
>
> *When the <u>finishing touches</u> are put on your "permission," you grab on to it like a man dying of thirst grabs at a canteen of water. Then here is what happens every time! There are always more than one in the "frame-up." The "frame-up" after much enthusiasm, conversation, advertising of prowess, getting together of broken suit cases and the usual flurry of an unusual trip, says—"Ah, we must now manage by hook or crook to get to Trèves, where we will all get sleeper reservations for Paris. We'll hang over there for about two days." The gang gets to Trèves—no reservations, no sleepers—no seats—very little standing room. The French have it all! About this time some guy with a "Bolshevik" spark in the back of his nut, says, more or less, "by the holy jumping bull-frog" we have these leaves and I'll be darned if we can be shoved out of a seat. The fire is started and off all go for at least a place on the train. All the aisles even are filled with "Frogs," bread and cheese. The outfit starts to board then the howl goes up—"Occupé" "Occupé!" "Reservé." The gang—"Reserve Hell" and the <u>Battle of Leave</u> is on. The first skirmish finds USA, seated, glowering, swearing and ready to stick a foot in the face of the first "Fwy" [slang: "F***ing with you"] who shows head in the door.*
>
> *No. 2. Nancy is reached after several hours hard ride. All are worn out. A brilliant idea hits me—"Let's get off and spend the night here"—"get that morning train." Without a word, baggage is grabbed—the door flung open, French jostled and stepped on and all are out in the Nancy station. An M.P. steps up—"Travel orders, please." And the record phase of the battle is on. No American soldier is allowed in Nancy —All kinds of papers must therefore be signed before you leave the station. There is no escape. You are wired in on all sides. When the A.P.M.*

[military for assistant program manager] *and M.P. turn you loose at the station with a hand full of <u>Don'ts and Do's</u> you feel like a bull at a bull fight. All hope of reserved seats for the next day are given up and all content themselves with the thought and <u>assurance</u> that seats will be secured by some method at the proper hour. Well, you ride all day from Nancy to Paris. Most of the conversation has reference to the <u>Paris stay</u>. Paris is reached and you find that there are strict orders that under no circumstance can one stay longer than between trains. Your leave is in Nice, and there you must go. The M.P.'s must then be out-done. The odds are all against you, but you take a chance. After missing one train, you then resume the operation of reaching Nice.*

One night and part of a day with experiences similar to the one from Trèves to Nancy and you reach Nice. Your troubles are now over for at least a week and you can freely enjoy the most beautiful spot anywhere. Sunshine, warm weather, beautiful hotels and plenty to <u>eat</u> of <u>every-thing</u>. I am back now and am glad I fought this great <u>battle</u>.

I paid Mr. House a visit on my way down. I saw him only a few minutes. He looked very well and was very glad to see me.

I did not get my money till I got to Nice—reached Paris on Saturday and had to leave Sunday.

Got your wire about seeing Mr. House about discharge. Got it here and therefore this was impossible. I have done everything I can from this end and maybe it will go through.

A communication from G.H.Q. quoted your telegram and asked for me to put in a request for discharge and reasons. I did so at once.

Got a letter from Raymond saying he was sailing. He came up to see me on the way home and we went to Paris together. He will no doubt see you before you get this.

My wound was nothing at all. I got a slight clip in the neck. Hardly a sign of it.

I see where they are going to reorganize the militia. I am sure I can get a regiment officered by 360th officers. If you get a chance to see Gov. Hobby, see if there is a chance for him to let me have this regiment. It will be the best in Texas.

I am very anxious to get home, and anything you can do—well, please do it.

With love -
Mike.

Cablegram to Will Hogg from Mike Hogg, March 26:

SAILING PRESIDENT GRANT
HOGG

On April 1, 1919, the President Grant docked at Newport News, Virginia. On April 2, Captain Mike Hogg sent a cablegram to his sister:

HOME AGAIN. MUCH LOVE.
MIKE

[GW] The 90th Division ceased to function as a division when it left Germany. . . .

The personnel of the 90th Division as soldiers, ceased to exist. The soul of the 90th Division continued and will remain (196).

The 90th Division's total casualties were 310 officers and 9,400 enlisted men. After the armistice in November 1918, the division moved into Germany for occupation duty. It was sent home for demobilization in May 1919.[61]

The enormity of the Great War was such that it came to be called the "War to End All Wars." That was in 1918.

Epilogue

For Henry Sheahan, George Wythe, and Mike Hogg, World War I left memories they would carry for the rest of their lives. After the war all three of these men went on to distinguished accomplishments in civilian life.

Henry Edouard Sheahan, born in Boston in 1888, spent his childhood in Quincy, Massachusetts. He attended Harvard, where he earned a BA degree in 1909 and a MA in 1911. In 1912–1913 he taught at the University of Lyon in France, and in 1914 returned to Harvard as an instructor in English. After the war, a few weeks after his return home, the *Boston Post* asked him to write some articles about his wartime experiences. The first article appeared on May 7, 1916. In July and August, the *Atlantic Monthly* published two of Sheahan's war articles, and these led to a book offer by Houghton Mifflin. *A Volunteer Poilu* appeared in October 1916. Sheahan went on to a literary career that included writing fairy tales (as Henry Beston), editing, teaching, and writing. Haunted for a time by his war memories, he moved in 1925 to a small house near the Atlantic Ocean and wrote his now-classic book about life on Cape Cod, *The Outermost House* (1928). This work later inspired environmentalists such as Rachel Carson. In 1929 Sheahan married Elizabeth Coatsworth (1893–1980), an author and poet. They had two daughters, Margaret, born in 1930, and Katherine, born in 1932. Sheahan and his wife lived for many years in Nobleboro, Maine, where he died at age eighty in 1968.

George Wythe, born in 1893 in Weatherford, Texas, was a descendant of the George Wythe who signed the Declaration of Independence. He attended the University of Texas and received a BA in 1912. When the war broke out, he was working as a journalist in Dallas, Texas. On April 26, 1917, Wythe enlisted in the US Army. Like Mike Hogg, he served in combat with the 90th Division during World War I. After the war, as Major George Wythe, he wrote the official history of his US Army division, the 90th, while in Germany in 1920. In 1924 he married Zoe Mostert (1903–1994). Wythe worked for the US Department of Commerce in the 1930s and earned a PhD in economics at George Washington University in 1938. As an expert on Latin America, he served as director of the American Republics section in the Department of Commerce until 1960. In 1972 he and his wife moved to Vienna, Austria, where he died in 1990 at age ninety-six.

Mike Hogg, who had earned a law degree from the University of Texas in 1911, returned to his oil-rich family's business interests in Houston after the war. In memory of the soldiers who had died in World War I, Mike, his brother, Will, and their sister, Ima, created Houston's fifteen hundred–acre Memorial Park. Opened in 1925, it is one of the largest urban parks in the United States. In 1927, at age forty-two, Mike Hogg entered politics, serving two terms in the Texas 40th and 41st Legislatures (1927–1931). In 1929 he married Alice Nicholson Fraser (1900–1977). He and his wife resided in Houston until Mike Hogg's death from cancer in 1941. He was fifty-six years old.

Notes

Preface

1. Translated from the French inscription. This is one of many images at "Pierre's Photo Impressions of the Western Front, 1914–1918," accessed April 24, 2017, http://pierreswesternfront.punt.nl/. Estimates of dead and wounded for World War I are difficult because of the deadly nature of trench warfare, and sources seldom agree. Laurence Stallings, *The Doughboys: The Story of the AEF, 1917–1918* (New York: Harper & Row, 1963), puts French casualties in this area from 1915 to 1916 at 125,000.

2. On the Battle of St. Mihiel, see Robert H. Ferrell, *America's Deadliest Battle: Meuse-Argonne, 1918* (Lawrence: University Press of Kansas, 2007), 32–39; Robert H. Zieger, *America's Great War: World War I and the American Experience* (New York: Rowman & Littlefield, 2000), 98–99; Stallings, *The Doughboys*, 213–19; Lonnie J. White, *The 90th Division in World War I: The Texas-Oklahoma Draft Division in the Great War* (Manhattan, KS: Sunflower University Press, 1996), 97–107; George Wythe, *A History of the 90th Division* (New York: 90th Division Association, 1920), 21–76.

3. Henry Sheahan, *A Volunteer Poilu* (Boston: Houghton Mifflin, 1916), 54–55. George Wythe wrote the official history of his US Army division, the 90th, while in Germany in 1920. Mike Hogg, who commanded troops in the 90th Division in the trenches of the Western Front, wrote letters home. Most of them were to his sister, Ima Hogg. On Henry Sheahan's life and career, see Daniel G. Payne, *Orion on the Dunes: A Biography of Henry Beston* (Jaffrey, NH: David R. Godine, 2016); and "About Henry Beston," 2010, http://www.henrybeston.com/about. html. George Wythe's biographical materials and military records are in the Wythe (George) Papers, Box 2.325/E497 [AR87–204], Dolph Briscoe Center for American History, University of Texas at Austin. For biographical information on Mike Hogg, see "Mike and Ima Hogg Papers, 1919–1972," MS19, accessed February 13, 2013, Archives, Museum of Fine Arts, Houston, http://fa.mfah. org/main.asp?target=eadidlist&id=79&action=3. See also Mike and Alice Hogg Papers, 1919–1972 (bulk 1930–1941), MS19, Archives, Museum of Fine Arts,

Houston; Mike Hogg Family, 1895–1976, Boxes 3B124 and 3B125, Ima Hogg Papers, Dolph Briscoe Center for American History, University of Texas at Austin. The Hoggs were a famous Texas family. J. S. Hogg was a colorful politician, and Ima was an arts patron and historic preservationist. See Robert C. Cotner, *James Stephen Hogg: A Biography* (Austin: University of Texas Press, 1959); and Virginia Bernhard, *Ima Hogg: The Governor's Daughter*, 3rd ed. (Denton: Texas State Historical Association, 2011).

Chapter 1

1. For general background on the war, see James L. Stokesbury, *A Short History of World War I* (New York: Morrow, 1981), which has become a standard. See also Edward M. Coffman, *The War to End All Wars: The American Experience in World War I*, 2nd ed. (Lexington: University Press of Kentucky, 1998); Zieger, *America's Great War*; David Burner, Virginia Bernhard, Elizabeth Fox-Genovese, et al., *Firsthand America: A History of the United States* (St. James, NY: Brandywine Press, 1991), 1:705–13.

2. American casualty figures are from "United States Military Casualties of War," accessed April 25, 2017, https://en.wikipedia.org/wiki/United_States_military_casualties_of_war.

Estimates vary. See "List of Battles by Casualties," Wikipedia, last modified March 17, 2017, https://en.wikipedia.org/wiki/List_of_battles_by_casualties. Zieger estimates the number of American dead at 60,000, with 206,000 wounded (*America's Great War*, xii, 108). Ralph A. Wooster, *Texas and Texans in the Great War* (Buffalo Gap, TX: State House Press, 2009), lists 32 million casualties and 4 million deaths during the war; the total American casualties were 364,000, including 120,000 dead from battle or disease (vii).The first American soldiers landed in France in June 1917, but major American involvement would begin in the spring of 1918 and continue through the Armistice of November 11, 1918. Coffman, *The War to End All Wars*, 3–4, 131–32; Jennifer Keene, *World War I*, Daily Life through History Series, American Soldiers' Lives, ed. David S. Heidler and Jeanne T. Heidler (Westport, CT: Greenwood Press, 2006), 15–21, 25.

3. Bernhard, *Ima Hogg*, 18–20.

4. Ima Hogg to Will Hogg, July 29, 1914, Box 3B125, Family Papers, Ima Hogg Papers, Briscoe Center for American History, University of Texas at Austin.

5. There is a good time line for the events of World War I from 1914 to 1920 in Zieger, *America's Great War*, xv–xxii.

6. Ima Hogg, Diary 1914, Box 4Zg86, Newspaper Clippings, Ima Hogg Papers; Ima Hogg to Will Hogg, August 4, 1914, Box 3B125, Family Papers, Ima Hogg Papers.

7. Ima Hogg to Will Hogg, August 25, 1914, Family Papers, Ima Hogg Papers.

8. Ima Hogg, Diary 1914.

9. "Battles: The First Battle of the Marne, 1914," firstworldwar.com, August 22, 2009, http://www.firstworldwar.com/battles/marne1.htm.

10. Adam Albright, "American Volunteerism in France," WWI, accessed April 25, 2017, www.gwpda.org/comment/volsamer.html.

11. "List of Battles by Casualties."

12. The American Field Service now operates a student exchange program for high school students to study abroad. Albright, "American Volunteerism in France." Steve Ruediger, "Prose & Poetry: Literary Ambulance Drivers," firstworldwar.com, August 22, 2009, http://www.firstworldwar.com/poetsand-prose/ambulance.htm; "Around Bois-le-Prêtre, the 'Forest of Death,'" accessed May 5, 2017, http://jmpicquart.pagesperso-orange.fr/ambtextGB.htm; A. Piatt Andrew, *Friends of France: The Field Service of the American Ambulance Described by Its Members* (New York: Houghton Mifflin, 1916); Leslie Buswell, *Ambulance No 10: Personal Letters from the Front* (New York: A. L. Burt, by arrangement with Houghton Mifflin, 1916); M. A. DeWolfe Howe, ed., *The Harvard Volunteers in Europe* (Cambridge, MA: Harvard University Press, 1916).

Chapter 2

1. Sheahan, *A Volunteer Poilu*, 7.

2. Ibid., 21–23. All excerpts quoted here are from this source and are hereafter cited parenthetically by page number in the text.

3. Hew Strachan, *The First World War* (New York: Viking, 2003), 181.

4. The field artillery guns that fired French 75's were also called by the same name. These cannons weighed four tons and needed a team of six horses to move them. One cannon could fire between fifteen and thirty rounds per minute—up to a distance of five miles. These "anti-personnel weapons" accounted for much of the terrible carnage of World War I. See "Canon de 75 modèle 1897," Wikipedia, last modified April 2, 2017, https://en.wikipedia.org/wiki/Canon_de_75_modèle_1897; and "The French 75: A New Gun for a New Century," Historical Society of the Georgia National Guard, accessed December 16, 2016, http://hsgng.org/legacy/pages/french75.htm.

5. On the "imperial" beard, see E. Cobham Brewer, *The Historic Note-book: With an Appendix of Battles* (Philadelphia: Lippincott, 1892), 82, https://books.google.com/books?id=YmwUAAAAYAAJ&pg=PA82&lpg=PA82&dq=Napoleon+III+whiskers&source=bl&ots=7AeK-t_cnZ&sig=0pc6gXF2°NqYn9W_avxuxAyHKhY&hl=en&sa=X&ved=0ahUKEwj6m6LBn9_MAhUN8WMKHVedDqsQ6AEISzAM#v=onepage&q=Napoleon%20III%20whiskers&f=false.

6. The author is Leslie Buswell, a young Englishman who was in the AFS in 1915. See *History of the American Field Service in France, 1914–1917*, accessed February 10, 2013, http://net.lib.byu.edu/estu/wwi/memoir/afshist/AFS1f.htm.

7. See "World War One BBC," accessed February 16, 2013, http://www.bbc.co.uk/history/worldwars/wwone/battle_verdun.html. This site gives the total French and German casualties each as 400,000.

8. "The Battle of Verdun and the Number of Casualties," The Battle of Verdun

1916, accessed February 4, 2013, http://www.wereldoorlog1418.nl/battlever-dun/slachtoffers.htm.

9. Henry Sheahan, "One of the Sections at Verdun," in Andrew, *Field Service of the American Ambulance*, V: *The Section in Lorraine*, http://www.gwpda.org/medical/FriendsFrance/ff02.htm. For the war writings of other ambulance drivers, see Ruediger, "Prose & Poetry."

10. Sheahan, "One of the Sections at Verdun."

11. Payne, *Orion on the Dunes*, 56.

12. Zieger, *America's Great War*, 22–29, 43–56, 60–61.

Chapter 3

1. On recruiting and training troops, see Keene, *World War I*, 33–37, 48.

2. On the organization of divisions, brigades, and regiments, battalions, and so on, see ibid., 129. On the history of the 90th Division and the 360th Regiment, see Victor F. Barnett, *A History of the Activities and Operations of the 360th United States Infantry in the World War, 1914–1918* (Zeltigen, Germany: Army of Occupation American Expeditionary Forces, 1919); White, *90th Division in World War I*.

3. Mike Hogg to Ima Hogg, May 1917, Box 3B125, Family Papers, Ima Hogg Papers. The originals of the letters are not extant. All of Mike Hogg's letters cited here are from the same source: Box 3B125, and can be located by date.

4. Bernhard, *Ima Hogg*, 82. Will Hogg to John Duncan, May 16, 1913. The graduation figures are taken from the First Officers Training Camp historical marker placed in Leon Springs. See "Leon Springs, Texas," TexasEscapes.com, accessed June 30, 2012, http://www.texasescapes.com/SouthTexasTowns/Le-on-Springs-Texas.htm#wwi. On training camps, see Coffman, *The War to End All Wars*, 25–29. Camp Funston, originally set up by Major General Frederick Funston, commander of the US Army Southern Department, who died in January 1917, became part of a plan to train thousands of combat-ready officers when World War I began. Funston had named this camp at Leon Springs for Cecil Lyon, a Texas politician who died in 1916, but most soldiers called it "Funston." It was to open on May 1, 1917. "Thousands to Train at Reserve School," *Galveston Daily News*, April 8, 1917; White, *90th Division in World War I*, 5, 18; "Leon Springs, Texas"; "Many Texans Get Commissions for Officers' Reserve," *El Paso Morning Times*, May 21, 1917.

5. Schofield Andrews to George Wythe, May 10, 1919, folder Correspondence, etc., Wythe (George) Papers, Box 2.325/E497 [AR87–204], Briscoe Center for American History.

6. Lonnie J. White, "Camp Travis," *Handbook of Texas Online*, accessed June 30, 2012, http://www.tshaonline.org/handbook/online/browse/index.html, uploaded on June 12, 2012, published by the Texas State Historical Association.

7. George Wythe, *History of the 90th Division*, 3. All excerpts from this source are hereafter cited parenthetically by page number in the text.

8. "History of Company D, 360th Infantry," typescript, undated, unpaged, private collection of Alan Garrett, Eastern New Mexico University.

9. James Stephen Hogg to Martha Frances Davis, September 16, 1888, James Stephen Hogg letter transcriptions and family photographs, MS 008, box 12, vol. 2, 56–62, Woodson Research Center, Fondren Library, Rice University.

10. Mike's new recruits were not atypical. Among the draftees of World War I, "most enlisted men had left school between the fifth and seventh grades." David M. Kennedy, *Over Here: The First World War and American Society*, 25th anniversary ed. (New York: Oxford University Press, 2004), 188.

11. "History of Company D."

12. Mike was not alone in having mumps: Camp Travis was full of sickness in the winter of 1917–1918: Pneumonia, measles, and mumps at the camp sent more than eight hundred men to bed. White, *90th Division in World War I*, 32.

13. The sweaters for Mike and his men were probably knitted by Houston women. Women's clubs, together with the Red Cross and other organizations, worked diligently to supply the troops with everything from items of clothing to surgical dressings. See May Harper Baines, ed., *Houston's Part in the World War* (Houston: n.p., 1919), 7–22, passim; Zieger, *America's Great War*, 141–42.

14. Mike Hogg to Will Hogg, April 24, 1918, "World War Letters, 1914–1918," Hogg Family Personal Papers, MS 21, Hogg Family Papers, Museum of Fine Arts Archives, Houston, Texas.

15. "History of Company D."

16. The British liner *Olympic*, carrying 6,100 soldiers, including Captain Hogg and his Company D, sailed for Europe on June 14, 1918, and arrived at Southampton, England, on June 21 after a smooth voyage. White, *90th Division in World War I*, 78–79.

17. Stallings, *Doughboys*, 26.

18. "History of Company D."

19. White, *90th Division in World War I*, 83.

20. On the St. Mihiel offensive, see Coffman, *The War to End All Wars*, 262–82; Ferrell, *America's Deadliest Battle*, 32–38.

21. "History of Company D."

22. Robert Whitney Imbrie, *Behind the Wheel of a War Ambulance* (New York: R. M. McBride, 1918).

23. White, *90th Division in World War I*, 97.

24. US infantry platoons were made up of twenty to forty enlisted men commanded by a lieutenant.

25. Sheahan, *A Volunteer Poilu*, 54–55.

26. "History of Company D."

27. American casualties were 7,000; German, 2,300. White, *90th Division in World War I*, 99.

28. "American Hand Grenades of W.W.I.," Inert-Ord.net, accessed May 13, 2016, http://inert-ord.net/usa03a/usa1/index.html.

29. Quoted in White, *90th Division in World War I*, 106, 107.

30. Ibid., 111.

31. "History of Company D."

32. The cartoon has not been found.

33. James A. Baker Jr. joined the army just before World War I and returned as a decorated war hero. His son, James A. Baker III, was secretary of the treasury under President Reagan and secretary of state under President George H. W. Bush. See "James Addison Baker: Steady Hand Shaped Success," *Houston Chronicle*, May 19, 2016, http://www.houstonchronicle.com/local/history/article/James-Addison-Baker-Steady-hand-shaped-success-7722733.php.

34. These figures are from Ferrell, *America's Deadliest Battle*, xi. See also J. Rickard, "Meuse River-Argonne Forest Offensive, 26 September–11 November 1918," HistoryOfWar.org, September 6, 2007, http://www.historyofwar.org/articles/battles_meuse_argonne.html. Casualty numbers vary. See George Thompson, "American Military Operations and Casualties, 1917–18," University of Kansas Medical Center, accessed December 28, 2016, http://www.kumc.edu/wwi/index-of-essays/american-military-operations-and-casualties.html, which gives a total casualty figure of 110,508 for the Meuse-Argonne battle. For a recent analysis, see Michael Nieberg, "The Battle of the Meuse-Argonne, 1918: Harbinger of American Great Power on the European Continent?," Foreign Policy Research Institute, May 9, 2012, http://www.fpri.org/article/2012/05/the-battle-of-the-meuse-argonne-1918-harbinger-of-american-great-power-on-the-european-continent/.

35. George W. Crile, quoted in Ferrell, *America's Deadliest Battle*, 39.

36. A "striker" was an enlisted soldier who cleaned an officer's uniform and sometimes prepared his meals. See "What Was a 'Stryker' in the 1870s US Calvary?," reddit AskHistorians, accessed April 26, 2017, https://www.reddit.com/r/AskHistorians/comments/3jkuff/what_was_a_striker.

37. The striker disappears from the letters. He did not come home with Mike.

38. "History of Company D."

39. Germany's spring offensive, a military effort to end the war on the Western Front, was sometimes called the "Peace Offensive." See "Germany Begins Major Offensive on the Western Front," History.com, accessed May 13, 2016, http://www.history.com/this-day-in-history/germany-begins-major-offensive-on-the-western-front.

40. "History of Company D."

41. Ibid.

42. Ibid.

43. Ibid.

44. Ibid.

45. Ibid.

46. Ibid.

47. Office of the Adjutant General to Will Hogg, November 6, 1918, "World War Letters, 1914–1918."

48. "History of Company D."

49. Ibid.

50. Barnett, *Activities and Operations of the 360th*, 151.

51. "History of Company D."

52. Ibid.

53. Ferrell, *America's Deadliest Battle*, 123.

54. General John J. Pershing to Major General Charles H. Martin, April 16, 1919, quoted in Barnett, *Activities and Operations of the 360th*, 6.

55. Ibid., 156, 159.

56. The Commission for Relief in Belgium was organized in 1914 to supply food to German-occupied Belgium, but it became an international relief agency in the war. Herbert Hoover, an American mining engineer who became president of the United States in 1928, was its director. See Commission for Relief in Belgium, accessed May 13, 2016, http://encyclopedia.1914–1918-online.net/article/commission_for_relief_in_belgium_crb.

57. Quoted in Barnett, *Activities and Operations of the 360th*, 6.

58. Document enclosed in the letter from Mike Hogg to Ima Hogg, November 14, 1918.

59. On the Army of Occupation, see White, *90th Division in World War I*, 164–172; Coffman, *The War to End All Wars*, 358–59. The 90th was one of eight US divisions selected for the Army of Occupation. Wooster, *Texans and Texas in the Great War*, 160.

60. See, for example, James Stephen Hogg's letters of October 21, 1894, and May 1, 1895, to his wife, Sallie, and to his daughter, Ima, April 19, 1895, with references to their friendship with Edward House and his family. Box 4Zg89, folder James Stephen Hogg Letters, 1895, Ima Hogg Papers. When Will Hogg died in 1930, Colonel E. M. House was one of the pall bearers at his funeral. Bernhard, *Ima Hogg*, 49, 84.

61. Casualty figures are from Dorman H. Winfrey, "Ninetieth Division," *Handbook of Texas Online*, accessed April 26, 2017, http://www.tshaonline.org/handbook/online/articles/qnn02, uploaded on June 15, 2010, published by the Texas State Historical Association.

Selected Readings

Andrew, A. Piatt. *Friends of France: The Field Service of the American Ambulance Described by Its Members*. New York: Houghton Mifflin, 1916.

Baines, May Harper, ed. *Houston's Part in the World War*. Houston: n.p., 1919.

Barnett, Victor. *A History of the Activities and Operations of the 360th United States Infantry Regiment in the World War, 1914–1918*. Zeltingen, Germany: Army of Occupation American Expeditionary Forces, 1919.

Bernhard, Virginia. *Ima Hogg: The Governor's Daughter*. 3rd ed. Denton: Texas State Historical Association, 2011.

Braim, Paul F. *The Test of Battle: The American Expeditionary Forces in the Meuse-Argonne Campaign*. 2nd ed. Shippensburg, PA: White Mane Publishing, 1998.

Buswell, Leslie. *Ambulance No 10: Personal Letters from the Front*. New York: A. L. Burt, by arrangement with Houghton Mifflin, 1916.

Coffman, Edward. *The War to End All Wars: The American Military Experience in World War I*. 2nd ed. Lexington: University Press of Kentucky, 1998.

Faulkner, Shawn. *The School of Hard Knocks: Combat Leadership in the American Expeditionary Forces*. College Station: Texas A&M University Press, 2012.

Ferrell, Robert H. *America's Deadliest Battle: Meuse-Argonne 1918*. Lawrence: University Press of Kansas, 2007.

Fussell, Paul. *The Great War and Modern Memory*. New York: Oxford University Press, 1975.

Grotelueschen, Mark. *The AEF Way of War: The American Army and Combat in World War I*. New York: Cambridge University Press, 2007.

Hallas, James H. *Squandered Victory: The American First Army at St. Mihiel*. Santa Barbara, CA: ABC Clio/Praeger, 1995.

Hansen, Arlen J. *Gentleman Volunteers: The Story of the American Ambulance Drivers in the Great War*. New York: Arcade Publishing, 1996.

Howe, M. A. DeWolfe, ed. *The Harvard Volunteers in Europe*: *Personal Records of Experience in Military, Ambulance, and Hospital Service*. Cambridge, MA: Harvard University Press, 1916.

Imbrie, Robert Whitney. *Behind the Wheel of a War Ambulance*. New York: R. M. McBride, 1918.

Jankowski, Paul. *Verdun: The Longest Battle of the Great War*. New York: Oxford University Press, 2014.

Keegan, John. *The First World War*. New York: Knopf, 1999.

Keene, Jennifer. *World War I*. Daily Life through History Series, American Soldiers' Lives. Edited by David S. Heidler and Jeanne T. Heidler. Westport: Greenwood Press, 2006.

Kennedy, David M. *Over Here: The First World War and American Society*. 25th anniversary ed. New York: Oxford University Press, 2004.

Lengel, Edward G. *To Conquer Hell: The Meuse Argonne 1918: The Epic Battle That Ended the First World War*. New York: Holt, 2008.

Nieberg, Michael. *Dance of the Furies: Europe and the Outbreak of War in 1914*. Cambridge, MA: Harvard University Press, 2011.

Paschall, Rod. *The Defeat of Imperial Germany*. Chapel Hill, NC: Algonquin Books, 1989.

Payne, Daniel G. *Orion on the Dunes: A Biography of Henry Beston*. Jaffrey, NH: David R. Godine, 2016.

Slotkin, Richard. *Lost Battalions: The Great War and the Crisis of American Nationality*. New York: Holt, 2005.

Stallings, Laurence. *The Doughboys: The Story of the AEF, 1917–1918*. New York: Harper & Row, 1963.

Stokesbury, James. *A Short History of World War I*. New York: Morrow, 1981.

Strachan, Hew. *The First World War*. New York: Viking, 2003.

Trask, David. *The AEF and Coalition Warmaking, 1917–1918*. Lawrence: University Press of Kansas, 1993.

Tuchman, Barbara. *The Guns of August: The Outbreak of World War I*. New York: Random House, 1962.

White, Lonnie J. *The 90th Division in World War I: The Texas-Oklahoma Draft Division in the Great War*. Manhattan, KS: Sunflower University Press, 1996.

Wooster, Ralph A. *Texas and Texans in the Great War*. Buffalo Gap, TX: State House Press, 2009.

Wythe, George. *A History of the 90th Division*. New York: 90th Division Association, 1920.

Zieger, Robert H. *America's Great War: World War I and the American Experience*. New York: Rowman & Littlefield, 2000.

Index